AF496768

IN THE SPIRIT

Tom Arild Fjeld

A new period of time - Global with signs, wonders and miracles - A greater conscious approach between the physical, the spiritual and the spiritual.

Preface

Pastor Dr. Morris Cerullo

It is with great humility and I consider it a great honor to write this foreword. Pastor Tom is the quintessential leader; a man after the heart of God, a man with a great calling, a man full of God's word and power, a great intercessor and a faithful soldier for Christ. His books were born out of a divinely inspired spirit deeply rooted in the Holy Scriptures, the Bible, the Word of God. Part of the devil's strategy is that he will cause us to live a poor life in defeat by neglecting the study of God's Word daily. That is why God has placed these great words in Pastor Tom to help His children gain more knowledge of Him and His kingdom. The power comes from what you know and how to use what you know to guide you into the revelation, guidance, and inspiration of the Holy Spirit. Follow Pastor Tom as he takes you on spiritual training sessions, on the spiritual training studio. You will be encouraged to believe God for the impossible. These books are a must for any believer who has an insurmountable desire to move and live on the next

level. You will get yourself aroused, to delve deeper into what is of God.
About the book It's awesome Brother Tom, I'm so glad that God gives you revelation and to write on the essence of what we need, to come forward with the living Word of God.

Remain forever blessed in Jesus name.

Dr. Morris Cerullo

Preface

What I have written in my book "Impact in the Spirit's World" I have included some of in this book. It is for a very special purpose. The area that deals with the realities of the spirit world and how to relate to it, I have mentioned in the above book with clarity.

In this book you are about to start reading, I will continue with this topic, but will delve deeper into it. I would, therefore, like to see the book "Impact in the spirit world" and this book you are now starting on called "In the Spirit", like 2 books that belong together.

These books will guide you into areas of the spiritual world, which are absolutely necessary, to live a victorious breakthrough life. Live the victorious life Jesus won for us on Calvary's cross.

The service

I have traveled in over 58 countries with the gospel, I started when I was 20 years old, I have met the devil and the resistance of demons in every nation I have been. It has taught me to deal with spiritual realities in many different ways in practical life.

You do not get to know the devil's snares and how to deal with them through books. It is learned only through practical experience in real life, in the fight against Satan and the demons. Take the Word of God seriously and step out of it, to win Christ, in the unreached areas of the physical world and in the spiritual world. You will gradually learn to live in victory, not just winning a battle, but winning the war.

The prayers.

Obsession

Going before God in the spirit and casting out demons of people possessed in their spirit. It is something one does not encounter so often ei- ther, either in the West or in the 3rd world.

Bound

What one sees a lot, however, is the unity of per- sonality, of the soul, where emotions, thoughts and will are. The headquarters in us for the soul is the brain, where our personality/soul is. Our soul is and is spiritual as our spirit but prioritized in different ways by God in us.

The brain is also a decoder of spiritual signals and words from God in the Spirit down to physical understanding in our mind.

Brain and heart are the same from Hebrew. They are called "Lab" Lab is the center of us, it is the center of communication in us spiritually and spiritually.

Oppression

There is often seen the suppression of demons from the outside and bands of demons on the inside in personality/soul. Both of these things are a lot.

Suppression from the outside can be solved without the help/cooperation of the needy.

When it comes to prayer in the deep and casting out demons of the bound, which are then on the inside, in the human soul/personality.

This is done in exactly the same way as suppression. The only difference is that when casting/casting demons out of the bound. This is done in direct cooperation with the aggrieved person.

If you go deep - go through it, it is a current situation in a process that you are tackling.

All this I teach in the chapters that follow. We can never manipulate a human being, the human being has his own free will, but it can be facilitated for the human being to have the opportunity to make a choice in the right direction and be free.

Are you willing?

I think this book contains just about everything in sobriety you need to be effective in the task I just mentioned. This is not a task for everyone but will be put on the heart of some and equipment will be provided

God for exercising this. Receiving equipment for such a service will cost you everything in your own life. Your life must be completely shut down for Christ. You will go through a cleansing and crushing process on the part of the Lord. It must be he who stands out in all and nothing and nothing of you.

Already here, there are many who are withdrawing from such a task for the kingdom of heaven. If you are willing to spend your entire life for

Him to spend the years needed to prepare for the task, then God needs you.

Warning

I want to warn dreamers, adventurous, sensation seekers, experts, and other proud personalities to move into the areas I will teach. If your motives are not right and your attitude humble before God and your fellow human beings, you should stay far away from this, so Satan does not attack you, as we have an example in Acts. 8,12-24 read all the verses myself, I just take something here: Simon came to the apostles with money to gain power.

The conversation Simon had with the apostles ended with him saying: Pray for me to the Lord that none of what you have said should come upon me.

We do not play with Satan, nor does he do with us. Not even the angel Michael dared to make a mocking judgment when he quarreled with the devil about Moses' body but said: The Lord punishes you (Jude 9).

I want to mention a serious case in it and not have respect for the spiritual realities.

The preacher Artur Cornelius told: Some students in the U.S.A. blindfolded a woman and led her - with her permission - into the prayer queue at Oral Roberts. She was going to pretend and be blind, and then the students would reveal Oral Roberts as a humbug maker when the woman proclaimed having regained her sight.

When the woman's turn came to pray, Oral Roberts could not raise his hand but stood in front of the woman who now took off the tie. Then a heartbreaking scream was heard from the woman: I have become blind. A little later in the meeting, Oral Roberts prayed for the woman and she regained her sight. As we see here - we are not playing with God. However, we stand with God, He stands completely with us.

The book

This book is a product of my own desire to write it and from requests, I have received through my television programs. It is written for those who simply want to understand how to "tear" the answers to the prayers out of the Devil's hands. I want this to be a "handbook" for you, a bit trendy, but I mean a handbook, which can be with you together with the Bible.

Satan and the demons

(Eph. 6:12) Here is written about the heavens above us and around us.

 The demons move throughout our atmosphere all over planet earth (Tellus). Satan's thoughts are shot out of the same areas. Satan and the demons are not yet in perpetual perdition, on the other hand, they fear perdition because they know that their day is coming, and they will be there forever and ever (John Rev. 20: 3 and 10). Our victory in Christ is an eternal fact. If we do not know our eternal victorious rights, then Satan holds on to what is rightfully ours. That is why the Bible says so clearly - do not give the devil room (Eph. 4:27). We do not when we know our rights in Christ and live them out.
This book is not for the "superficial prayers without prayer answers" -
but for the "deep prayers, which tear the answer out of Satan and the grip of demons".
Satan has our rights in his grasp to the extent that we do not know our rights in Christ, and with our rights, our victory rips out of Satan's hands.

Satan and the demons have woven into the world of mankind as one woven rug
Satan has infiltrated himself with his demons in this world like a blanket woven with human threads and demonic and satanic threads. Imagine the infiltration of demons that have grown since Adam and Eve and the fall of the Garden of Eden (Gen.3)

The victory is ours in Christ Jesus
Never discuss with Satan or the demons, victory is our unconditional. Close your ears to his accusations and condemnations, never be intimidated by his threats. all he says is just a lie (John 10:10). No matter how much demonic activity there is, our unconditional victory.

Identify yourself and your enemy
Carry your prayers soul's anguish and anguish, carry your prayers child out in freedom. As far as possible, take your bean topic space.

Use your God-given authority in the name of Jesus without a doubt (James 1,6-8)
In the trials and teachings, you will now go through, you will face many confrontations,

which will require you to know carefully and seriously whether it is God, is it myself, or is it Satan. This cannot be learned by reading, only by
experience, time after time, in the end, you understand it and you have it.

Not the gift of discernment of spirits, but because you have been involved and taught, you,
as a mature Christian (as all Christians should be
with time, walking with the Lord), discern the
spirits of the heat of battle.
Good luck with your study and pursuit of this
subjects

Author
Tom Arild Fjeld

CONTENTS

I belived it - but it hasn't been fully real to me

Innate imagination

As humans, we are human beings, created in the image of God. Our creation has been limited in our "room", in our existence, as a result of the Fall.

"He has done everything in His time though; He has also put eternity in their hearts, but so that man cannot fully understand the work God has done from beginning to end. " (Ecc. 3, 11)

Man had great limitations. Science talks about using only 1/10 of the brain, to what extent it's right, I don't know.
But we still have many talents and gifts in operation, of varying degrees of strength in people.

The ability to imagine things

This is a gift we have inborn, which also differs in strength in all of us. It is the ability to imagine things, to define things that are not immediately "discovered". As you know, women have a stronger intuition than men. We have all through our ancestors, Adam and Eve, inherited intuition, which we call it in modern language. Adam and Eve had all abilities fully developed before the Fall.

That being said, there is nothing intuitive about Adam and Eve. But it is an ability we know today that we must assume was in them too. After the fall, we see that there was a great restriction on man in all areas, including on what we call intuition. It may seem that intuition is somewhat recognizable in relation to the "ability" to test spirits. But the "ability" to try spirits is of deeper quality. That ability is exercised by surrendering to the Lord and using it.

The ability to discern spirits

"Another power to do wonders, another prophetic gift, another ability to test spirits, another different kind of tongues, another interpretation of tongues." (1Cor. 12.10)

In various car translations / basic texts, this verse reads as follows: "Ability" to "try" in Norwegian Bible, "discern" in King James and "see" from Greek. This is not a gift of grace, but an "ability" we all have.

It can be developed through repentance, surrender, study of Scripture, and obedience in practical action, at the commandments and promises of the written Word of God. Through this exercise, this will develop. This is nothing to be gained by the laying on of hands.

Only the path of obedience counts here, the obedience of the Lord and His written Word, the Bible.

To explain this ability easily,
I can say:
If you have been married for many years, you know your spouse in most areas. If someone comes to imagine that someone else is your spouse, you automatically reveal it. Here's how it is. The closer you get to Christ, the quicker you discern, or are able to try, spirits (as the Norwegian Bible calls it).

Important for your entire spiritual development

This ability is important for you to have, for the development of your own spiritual life. It will help you make the right choices before God. This will also be an opener to draw closer to the Lord, and into a deeper fellowship with Him.

You need this "ability" badly

When the Lord speaks quietly to you to draw you closer, Satan's thoughts do the same - he whispers thoughts to you. You see, you need this ability badly.

Development of ability: A spiritually strong life and character go hand in hand

The ability will not help you unless you believe in it - and act actively on it. As this ability develops, your character develops. This goes hand in hand. By imagining yourself or others that you have this, it will be revealed whether you have it or not - by your behavior and understanding. God has put "fuses" into all spiritual reality! **After the discovery / revelation comes the faith that is guided by the will.**

After the "thing" has been defined, we can believe the "thing" into reality. Within the limits set beforehand by God and His creative power. Man can do this with his free will.

This can be used for both good and evil. When we understand this, we see that

The "subject of battle" in the spiritual warfare is who is to define reality.

God's Word or contemporary illusions

I include a quote from the Bible that illustrates this wonderfully:

"So, as we have not the visible to the eye, but the invisible, for the visible is temporal, but the invisible is eternal." (2 Cor. 4-18)

We can understand in this verse that Paul had become familiar with the methodology of realization in the spiritual world, based on the methodology in the physical world.

The physical world

Here's an example: You get to see and touch a book for one second. You then close your eyes - and visualize in your inner person what you saw

6

with your physical eyes (for one second), and physically touch it with your hands. Now you see the color, size, shape and feel of the book. Here you get a visualization from the physical world, into your personality / soul, into your thought life - through physical senses.

The spiritual world and its functioning
Now we go out into the spiritual world. There you hear words from the world of the Spirit, from the world of the Holy Spirit of God. You hear words from the Holy Spirit world come to your thinking, to your intellect. Furthermore, you visualize the thoughts and you see them in your mind.

The psalmist says, "I will open my mouth with the language of thought." (Psalm 78: 3)

Daniel says, "The vision, the words, and the dreams through the head" (Daniel 7, 1-2)

You will get a visualization of the words of the Holy Spirit in your thinking and in your emotional life, in your soul. This comes via your thinking and emotional life. Further through the actions of faith, into the physical, sensory world. The recipient from the physical world and the spiritual world, is the thought life, and the emotions in our soul / personality.

Common recipient

Here we have a common recipient both from the physical side and the spiritual side. For both sides must be made alive in our souls.

Physical actions

We act in faith in the thoughts which are in accordance with the word of God. That in order for the thoughts to become a reality in the physical world.

Soulful actions

What goes into the spiritual through the presence of God, Jesus Christ and the Holy Spirit - we act on faith, we exercise faith in practical actions. This happens through the soul / in the mind - again for doors to enter the spiritual. This always happens by casting out evil spirits and healing the sick in Jesus' name. This is spiritual warfare.

8

Faith is the high threshold

Both on the physical and the spiritual side it is the threshold of the spiritual faith we must overcome. The soul is the door out of physical reality and into the spirit world. We walk through the same door from the spirit world to the physical reality. Your faith opens this door both ways.

NB!

Information for Chapters 2 and 3

These chapters provide information that has not been significantly known in Christian circles. We as Christians have, as I see it, for many generations "hung up" in the spiritual. Spiritism and the occult have always used the spiritual world. It is a reality that the spiritualist and the occult work in the spiritual world on the black side. Satan has given them the opportunity for a limited entrance in this area. When alternative fairs are arranged, the spiritual is immediately promoted. The New Age movement has been a major driver in this area, especially through one of its leaders and founders named David Spangler. We are in a truly spiritual battle and victory is ours.

God has given us the full entrance and understanding of the whole spiritual world through the revelation of His Word.

In the next two chapters I will give you some information in this area. We are saved who are to lead — along with God our Father and Jesus Christ.

Prayers That Reach Further Up than to the Roof

Our prayer life must reach a level that touches the realities of the spiritual world and can create a change there.

How does what you visualize in your thinking life materialize in the physical world?
"Jesus said, go out into all the world and preach the gospel to all creation." (Mark. 16. 15-18)

This was the last thing Jesus said to His disciples before His ascension. It was also the most important thing He said about our mission for Him, who gave birth to Christians on earth. I've always divided verse 15 into two parts.

1: Go out into the world
2: Preach the gospel to all creation

Now we go deeper into the verse. It goes with the words: "Go out into the world." We can never use the Bible's basic language enough. There are inexhaustible truths.

"Go out," in this verse, means the community (singular) to go out. That means this applies to absolutely everyone. The word also has to give and do good. We can also see in Hebrews 13:16 that the same Greek word is used. The word here means Joint participation and charity.
The command is for you. We see in this verse clearly that Jesus is talking about you, as a reborn individual, making your part of the command. This is not a request from Jesus, but a command to you. Let's keep this in mind **as we move on to the word "world". This is then from Greek and Latin translation.**

Cosmos

The cosmos is the Greek and Hebrew word for the universe/cosmos, these words are used synonymously.

"World". The word is called in Greek and Hebrew: Cosmos, which in turn translated into Norwegian means: Bring, come, follow, order, system, harmony, the universe, the world, eternity, forever, wipe out time in memory (past and future, in practice, is this eternity), time and eternity. Not limited to the present.

"Come your kingdom"
This meaning is also found from Greek in Matt. 6:10: "Come Thy Kingdom." The spiritual reality, the kingdom of God and the kingdom of heaven, is the same at times, but not always. At the end of human history, these two will forever be one.

The world is the whole cosmos

The world we live in is vast and boundless. The human race is limited and lives in a small part of the world.

Mankind is aware of the existence of other planets/galaxies, as well as other things in the universe/cosmos. Science says the cosmos has certain elements. It is: Time, vacuum, space, matter, and energy. These are things that then take place. Furthermore, the physical laws, which govern this which has then been constant throughout its history.

Do not understand (will not, cannot)

Mankind lives on the planet Tellus, which is like a little seed in a world (the spiritual) that is the whole cosmos, with the physical elements that are in it.

Science has seen some of it all, with the glasses of evolution. The little they have observed is correct, but they do not (will not, cannot) see the absolute bulk of the world.

The entrance to the spiritual world goes through the new birth

The entrance is spiritual and the first step of the entrance there is through the new birth - and a humble surrendered life to Christ Jesus.

"We do not have what is visible to the human eye, but what is visible to the spiritual eye. The invisible eye can only be seen by a human that is born again and live a surrendered life to Jesus. Everything visible is temporal, but the invisible is eternal". (2 Cor. 4:18)

One day, this planet we live on disappears from the world - and it becomes a new earth. John saw this in a view of the island of Patmos. The Bible says about this:

"And I saw a new heaven and a new earth; for the first heaven and the first earth were gone, and the sea is no more. " (Rev. 21.1)

A spiritual priority in our lives

One day, our physical reality will be gone forever. From then on, humanity will only be the spiritual world (either on Satan's side or on God's side). Until that day we have both the physical and the spiritual side. Here, one choice today seems to be simple: Namely, to choose Christ Jesus as Lord and enter into God's plan in time! Then the spiritual life of the world / cosmos must be given a first priority in our lives. This gives a completely different weight, size and understanding of Mark 16.15. " Each one should go into the cosmos - which is the spiritual and the physical world."

1. The gospel to the whole world so that Jesus can come again

What we have understood most often in this verse is that the gospel should reach out to all unreached people so that Jesus can come again. It is one part of our task on the little seed of a globe, Tellus, in the cosmos. We have been concerned about this and it is absolutely correct. It is this task that I have also been aware of throughout my adult life.

A task of participation and charity for the unreached with the gospel. We will continue to do so until Jesus comes again. This is part of the march from Christ. This was Jesus' last command before He went to heaven.

2. Personal fellowship with the Trinity

The second meaning of the word cosmos that opened to me is as follows: In all the years I have sought to draw ever closer to the Lord. It ended with a breakthrough. It brought me into areas brand new to me. After the beginning of the new pervasive experiences, I have sought Scriptural approval of it, and received it.

God's written Word is our only guideline, everything should be consistent with it

The beginning of a new life with the Lord, the triune God Jehovah.

Here are some encouraging verses: "I love those who love Me, and those who seek Me, will find Me." (Proverbs 8.17)

"And ye shall seek Me, and ye shall find Me when ye seek Me with all your heart" (Zech. 29:13).

"The Lord is good to those who wait on Him, to the soul who seeks Him." (Lamentation 3.25)

"For thus saith the LORD unto the house of Is-rael, Seek me, and ye shall live. Seek the good and not the evil, and you will live. Then the Lord, the God of hosts, will be with you, as He said! " (Amos 5.14)

Can We Get Clearer in Scripture? Let this be the beginning of a new life with the Lord for you. Let's move on.

Our fight.

Here it is good to mention Paul's words to the Ephesians:
"We are not fighting against powers, against authorities, but against the spirit armies of evil in the heavens." (Eph. 6:12)

The total cosmos is our field of work
Here in the letter to the Ephesians it is not just talk of our near sky / atmosphere being alone, is 100 km thick and extends towards the universe. The farther we get up from the earth's surface, the thinner the air becomes and the less is pressed down to the ground. Up here, the air is extremely thin. Then 99.99% of the atmosphere is at the bottom of these 100 km.

The Border to room – the space of our universe

Many consider this to be the border with space. Here, in a way, is the "roof" of the planet Tellus that we live on. Outside the "roof" is the space of our universe. Outside our planet and its atmosphere, out of our galaxy, past 100 billion galaxies in our universe - science has recorded the most distant galaxy in our universe. It is 13 billion light years away!

According to scientists, our universe is almost completely empty. Then we understand some of the distances and sizes.

The cosmos holds all universes

Outside our universe, there are new universes. Now we talk about the cosmos that all universes are in, plus everything else that we will never have any understanding or knowledge of. New theories mind you - theories - suggest that there may be many other universes that we can never know about.

Where is God Jehovah's heaven?

19

Bible Measurement Unit

"Height, length, breadth, and depth" (Eph. 3:18)
The spiritual and eternity.
The Bible has a unit of measurement called
"eternal, eternity." Even scientists have used
these measurement terms and one more unit of
measurement, which is even more extensive than
this one.

God's consciousness

It says it all, and everyone consists of stardust.
Consciousness exists from eternity to eternity,
with the intention of developing into cosmic
consciousness, and later the consciousness of
God. The word God is used as the strongest unit
of measurement.
Eternity is Abolished in All They do not understand what they are talking about, but eternity is
abolished in all, Ecclesiastes 3, 11, so certain
things "skip" without understanding the depth of
what they are talking about. It is God's infinite
wisdom that must enter the path. Only those who
are born again and live a surrendered life to the
Lord Christ Jesus have the opportunity to see
and understand this. (More about this in my
book: "Dressed Up for Victory").

To all the world

Our mission and command from Christ apply "to all the world." Thus, the present physical world we know of. To put it in a simpler and more understandable way: We reach out to all unreached people with the gospel while seeking God out of our inner spiritual lives.

Going Into the Lord - Alone (Don't Give Up)

The only way for us to make contact with eternity is to act purposefully, obediently, and in faith in God. By embarking on this task toward a close fellowship with the Godhead, we continue our quest, Matt. 6, 6. We never give up on this walk. It will seem to you like everything is closed. You see no progress. The secret lies in trusting the Lord's Word.

Be bold

"Let us therefore come forth boldly to the throne of grace, that we may have mercy and find grace to help in due time." (Heb. 4.16)

Go ahead with boldness, boldness, perseverance, confidence in your confidence in the Word of God, no matter what the circumstances will tell you through your senses.

Listen to this verse in the Preacher: "Everything God has done in His time; eternity / world / cosmos is also put into their hearts, but so that man cannot fully understand the work of God, from beginning to end. " (Ecclesiastes 3, 11)

Part of the Cosmos is in us A part of the cosmos is in all people (Genesis 1:26), one must just have to surrender one's life to Jesus Christ so that one can enter into the fullness of the spiritual.

4

The shepherds, angels, and armies

The shepherds out in the fields

"In the area that they were shepherds and over-saw their flock by night, an angel of the Lord appeared to them, and the glory of the Lord appeared around them, and they were greatly dismayed.

The angel said to them, "Do not be afraid; For behold, I preach unto you a great joy, which shall come unto all the people.

You are today born a Savior who is Christ the Lord in the City of David.
And this is to your sign: You will find a child wrapped in a manger.

And immediately there was with the angel a heavenly army (host), who promised God and said:

Glory be to God in the highest, and peace on earth, in man his good pleasure!

And it happened when the angels had gone from them to heaven, then
 the shepherds said to one another, "Let's go to Bethlehem now and see what has happened and as the Lord has told us!"

And they hurried and came and found both Mary Joseph and the child lying in the crib.
And when they had seen it, they told them the word that had been told them about this child.

And all who heard it wondered at what was said to them by the shepherds.

But Mary hid all these scents, however, because of them in her heart.
And the shepherds went back, praising and praising God for all that they had heard and seen, as they were told.

And when eight days came to an end, and he was to be circumcised, he was called Jesus, the name that the angel had mentioned before he was conceived in the womb. " (Luke. 2, 8-21) Read all the verses in context.

The shepherds in the field had never seen an angel alive.

Nor had they ever looked into the spiritual world. A spiritual experience like this was completely unknown to them. They must have been greatly shocked out there in the fields when the angel suddenly stood in front of them and spoke to them. This was beyond their grasp.

The angel had come from another dimension, from the fourth dimension. The most real dimension of all creation.

God's own world, the world that was before all other things Out there where all the universes, galaxies, stars, and planets were created by His Word.

Everything that is has come from a spiritual reality in the fourth dimension. This dimension is the most real dimension in the entire creation.

The world of God

This is God's own world. The world that was before anything else was. Lead the universes, galaxies, stars, and planets. Those who were all created by God's own spoken Word. Everything has come from an invisible world for the human senses. An invisible world, for we who eventually lived in a three-dimensional world, a physical world, under physical laws. A world that is recorded through physical senses. The world of the Spirit having its own laws.

From that reality, the angel had come to visit the shepherds. The angel spoke with a voice they could hear and with words they could understand. The angel gave them a message. Here, the angel manages to convey messages with words audible from the spirit world to the physical world. How it happened, I do not understand. What I want to show is that there is another world outside of the physical, with which we, as reborn humans, want to have a strong relationship and cooperation.

The angel said in audible words
"And immediately there was with the angel a heavenly host, who praised God, saying,

Glory be to God in the highest, and peace on earth, in man his goodwill

And it happened when the angels had gone from them into heaven…" (Luke. 2, 13 - 15)

Which of the shepherds or you today can understand this?

In and out of the spiritual and physical world
This is God working and we accept it or not.
This is a powerful miracle for us, humans, from God; It is in this way that he works. In and out of the spiritual world and the physical world.

The kingdom of God has come to earth?
 "Jesus said to his disciples: If it is by the Spirit of God, I cast out the evil spirits, then the kingdom of God has come to you." (Matt. 12:28)

You see or understand in the physical, Jesus was there in the natural human world, the physical world, the three-dimensional world while working in the spiritual world.

The angel came to the shepherds in the field in exactly the same way. Out of the fourth dimension (the spiritual world) and into the third dimension (the physical world)

So you see - after the redemption work of Jesus Christ on Calvary, victory was everywhere. Satan and the work of the demon a reality. Jesus won the victory for you. You can enter this world of reality; you can live in the physical and the spiritual at the same time.

Celestial Army Hosts
Another thing happened here, which is often overlooked and not understood.

"And immediately there was with the angel a heavenly army," (Luke 2, 13)

What is the Celestial Army (Host)?

In Genesis, we see those opening themselves for the first time." Then heaven and earth with all their army were completed." (Genesis 2, 1)

I give you simple credible assurance regarding this. We are born again believers of Jesus Christ, who live in the arena of victory - in the total victory forever.

An army of horses and wagons around the city

See here in 2 Kings: "And when the servant of this man of God went early in the morning, he saw an army of horses and chariots encircling the city. And his boy said unto him, O my Lord, what shall we do?

He answered, "Don't be afraid!" Those who are with us arc more than those who are with them. And Elisha prayed, saying, Lord! Open his eyes so he can see! And the Lord opened the boy's eyes, and he saw that the mountain was full of fiery horses and chariots all around Elisha. And when the Syrians came down unto him, Elisha prayed unto the LORD, saying, Smite these people blindly. And he struck them with blindness, as Elisha had asked" (2 King 6, 15-17)

Let's move on.

Let's read from Matthew: "And Jesus was declared before their eyes, and his face shone like the sun, and his clothes became white as the light.

And behold, Moses and Elijah appeared unto them, and spoke unto him,

While he was still speaking, there came a bright cloud and overshadowed them, and behold, a voice came out of the cloud, and said, this is my beloved Son, in whom I am well pleased; hear him! " (Matt. 17, 2-3 and 5)

Here again, we see some of the heavenly armies and the voice of Almighty God Jehovah, or as the English language puts it, "hosts." Here spiritual realities are realized in the physical world. They heard the voice with their physical senses, their ears and they saw things they could not see with their eyes.

The word "Host"
This word has no clear definition in translations or in the Bible. What I get out of this word, as I have studied it a bit, is as follows: A heavenly army.

Things that "are", not "created"
Hosts are "hosts", which means "beings" Here is not the word creature inside the picture.

Here are just a few things. In my simple understanding, I would say that there are angels present, beings, that is, another type of personalities that are not creatures in our understanding. I believe and the spirit army of evil, that is, the demons were behind and watching these groundbreaking events in the Old Testament and in the transition to the New Testament. They were and are all alone in the spirit world.

See here: "As they went and talked together, there came at once a glowing chariot and glowing horses and separated them; and Elijah was in the storm up to heaven. " (2 King 2, 11)

The revelation of the spirit in the natural in the Old Testament
Can you see it? The power of Almighty God was powerfully present. The same power of God is here today, only even stronger.

The reason for this is the Atonement that was completed perfectly by Jesus Christ on Calvary. All of this will be with you as you step out to obey the Lord's command.

It may seem that the "rooms" are security guards from God, who stay a little in the background. They come forward when needed. Most likely they have a type of angel standard.

The overall importance of faith - nothing works except through faith

Another important thing to be clear about is - nothing works without faith.

Listen: all things are possible for the believer

1 Believe in the victory of Jesus Christ,

2 believes in the New Testament promises, as a result of the   perfect reconciliation work on Calvary.

3 Believe in the effect of using the name of Jesus.

Jesus said, "If you can? All things are possible to the one" (Mark 9:23)

NB!

Those with Divine revelation and authority can go in and out - in faith

The Bible says, "But faith is full certainty of what is hoped for, conviction of things not seen." (Heb. 11: 1)

The authority in the voice of God can be in your voice and you can see everything He wants you to see.

Angel Revelations in Sala Polivalenta, Bucharest, Romania

On several occasions, there have been angel revelations in my meetings around the world. I will mention one episode. In Sala Polivalenta, Romania's largest indoor sports hall in the capital Bucharest. There, angels appeared behind me. Jesus also revealed himself behind me at the same time. It was at one of the meetings with the crowded hall this happened. I didn't see it, but the whole hall saw it at the same time. When I was going to pray for the sick at the end of the meeting, it happened. People started pointing and talking in the hall, I didn't understand what they were saying.

It was translated by the interpreter, I just stood still on the platform. They saw Jesus standing behind me with my hands on my shoulders as I began to pray for the sick. On each side of me, they saw angels.

I didn't see it, but many thousands said they saw Jesus and angels, so what can I say then. Then it must have been so.
What I saw when I commanded demons to come out was black smoke rising from the crowd in different places.

This tells me that the Kingdom of Heaven, the Divine Spiritual Kingdom was present. This again shows me that this is fully possible for us to live together in the Spiritual world of God today.

5

Angels and armies (beings) came down from heaven and went back to heaven again

I'll say it again
The angels and armies moved back again, through the divine gate to heaven. Through the heavenly doors from the physical world to the spiritual world.

We see the armies of heaven appearing on earth for the first time.
"Then heaven and earth with all their army were perfected." (Genesis 2, 1)

We also see it revealed to the shepherds in the field
In Luke we see: "And immediately there was with the angels a heavenly host who promised God." (Luke. 2, 13)

Here it was not only the angels who revealed
themselves, but also a heavenly army.
This is often overlooked and not understood.
Now it is obvious to you and understood by you.

Isn't it exciting to get along, like here in Luke:

"And it happened when the angels had gone
from them into heaven." (Luke. 2:15)

Then the angels left them and ascended to heav-
en again
Isn't it interesting to observe? The angels went
back to heaven, not just into the world of the
spirit.

 2 Kings says: "As they went and talked together, there came at once a fiery chariot and glowing horses and separated them; and Elijah was in
the storm up to heaven. " (2 King 2, 11)

2 Kings says further: "And when the servant of
this man of God departed early in the morning,
he saw an army of horses and chariots encircling
the city. And his boy said unto him, O my Lord,
what shall we do?

He answered, "Don't be afraid!" Those who are with us are more than those who are with them.

And Elisha prayed, saying, Lord! Open his eyes so he can see! And the Lord opened the boy's eyes, and he saw that the mountain was full of fiery horses and chariots all around Elisha.
And when the Syrians came down unto him, Elisha prayed unto the LORD, saying, Smite these people blindly. And he struck them with blindness, as Elisha had asked
He answered, "Don't be afraid!" Those who are with us are more than those who are with them.
And Elisha prayed, saying, Lord! Open his eyes so he can see! And the Lord opened the boy's eyes, and he saw that the mountain was full of fiery horses and chariots all around Elisha.

And when the Syrians came down unto him, Elisha prayed unto the LORD, saying, Smite these people blindly. And he struck them with blindness, as Elisha had asked. " (2 King 6, 15-18)

Jesus were transfigured to the disciples' eyes
Let's move on. Let's take a bit back from Matthew, what we read earlier:

"And Jesus was explained to them. His face shone like the sun, and his clothes were white as the light. " (Matt. 17, 2-3 and 5)

Our sign of assurance is "Jesus"
We can move like this, but it requires closeness to the Lord, and a lot of training that provides experience.

We can move like this in the spirit world as we live close to the Lord, train ourselves and gain experience. The only sure sign for us is that we have Jesus as truly Lord in our lives and that we then live filled and guided by the revealed Spirit of the written Word of God to us personally.
Now you got it again.

The spiritual reality has been from eternity (Cosmos, Greek)
The spiritual world has been, yes, has been in eternity in time and space, before us. And for eternity it will be with us and after us. This reality is with us right now.
In Jesus Christ, we can get into a much more intimate relationship with the reality of life, more

than we ever thought possible. It is boundless forever what God has available to us at all times.

Even the evil spirits obey us in your name
"And the seventy came back gladly, saying, Lord! Even the evil spirits obey us in your name!

Then Jesus said to them, I saw Satan fall from heaven like a lightning bolt.

Behold, I have given you power to tread upon serpents and scorpions, and overall, the power of the enemy, and nothing shall harm you.
But do not rejoice in the fact that the spirits are obedient to you but rejoice that your name is inscribed in heaven!

At that very moment, Jesus rejoiced in the Holy Spirit, and said, I praise thee, Father, Lord of heaven and earth, because thou hast hid it from the wise, and understanding, and revealed it to the unbelieving; yes, Father, because thus it happened that was pleasing to you. "
(Luke. 10, 17-21)

They understood some of what was hard to believe
The disciples understood something, but they did
not have the Spirit of revelation. They were not
born again. They had heard the story of the
shepherd's experiences in the field, they had experienced Jesus' Divine intervention many times
and now this. They understood some of what
was hard to believe.

Jesus is transfigured on the mountain
I just want to mention something again for this
experience.

"And behold, Moses and Elijah appeared unto
the disciples and talked with him.

While Jesus was still speaking, they, there came
a bright cloud and overshadowed them, and behold, a voice came out of the cloud, so he said:
This is my beloved Son, in whom I am well
pleased; hear him!

But when they looked up, they saw no one without Jesus alone

And as they went down from the mountain, Jesus commanded them, "Tell no one about this vision until the Son of Man has risen from the dead." (Matt. 17, 3-9) Read the entire verse.

Following Jesus' resurrection from the dead, and the disciples being reborn and baptized in the Holy Spirit, the opportunities to enter the reality of revelation were present, just as it is for us today. But it requires that we seek the Lord with all our heart, until we reach the spirit world forever and ever, yes in all eternity.
Not a quest with many words, but with a devoted heart.

6

You can do it

Do you live your life surrendered and converted to Christ so that the deeds of the flesh have been laid off and are at a laid-back stage in your life? And your spiritual growth is in progress, so the fruits of the Spirit have become a reality in your life.

Then you are ready for the next step into the reality of the Spirit.

The door of the senses must be closed
It is the Spirit of God through your spirit that will provide information and guidance to your soul, to your intellect and your feelings.

Something is to be exercised through your senses to the physical world, while other things are to be processed in the spiritual world.

Never give up.
The path you are about to take is a necessary course of learning. Without that hike you never reach.

Here is the walk in a nutshell
Hear what Paul said.

"So that I may know him (not the knowledge of), Jesus, and the power of his resurrection, and the fellowship of his sufferings, being made equal to him in his death," (Phil. 3:10).

You will gradually be led with your life, into a knowledge of God, a life you did not know existed. It will be you and the reality of the Godhead alone. God, Himself will teach you the way. Remember that everything must be following the written Word of God at all times. As you can see it will require everything from you. You must be in God's training camp until it sits. Obeying, learning and experience is one that applies.
Peter in prison
In the Acts, we have the story of Peter being imprisoned. It didn't look like much to him.

"At this time King Herod laid hands on some of the congregation and mistreated them."
(Acts. 12: 1-3)

These are things that are not noticed as much as we read the Bible. Here, some members of the congregation were abused and tortured for their faith in Jesus. Jacob, John's brother, was killed with a sword. This was a horrible situation. When Herod and his conspirators saw that these were pleasing to the Jews, they also seized Peter and imprisoned him. This was not long after the Atonement of Jesus Christ on Calvary. The victory was already won by Jesus, but see what happens anyway ...
This is something to think about.

Sincere prayer
Let's go to Peter who was imprisoned.
(Acts. 12,4.5)

In verse 5 we see that the congregation was in "deep prayer" for Peter. It does not help with heartfelt prayer when that prayer is only unbelief, doubt, and fear.

The type of prayers that don't reach longer up than the ceiling

We see Peter coming out of prison with the help of angels! (v 7.8) When Peter sat in prison, he sat there with the expectation of faith that the Christ he served would get him out of prison! And it happened! Peter even believed Jesus for his deliverance from prison. If head, he had not done so; he would have remained there in prison until he was executed.

" The angels led Peter here through the first guard and the second guard. " (v 10.11)

The "obedience of faith " works through the use of will power everybody have

Here Peter could have let his faith sink as he saw one obstacle after another. Instead - with his will - he walked in the obedience of faith until God brought him out. "Then they went through the first guard and the second, and came to the iron gate which led out to the city; It opened to them by itself, and they stepped out and went up a street, and immediately the angel parted from him. "

Had Peter not been faithful, these things would not have happened

On the other hand, if we are firm in the faith, if we are established in the faith, things will happen more and more powerfully around us. Like here with Peter. After he got out of prison (v 12) we see Peter go to the house where the "heartfelt prayer" had been prayed. And they still prayed.

.

"And when Peter knockcd on the gate, a maid named Rode came out to listen. And when Rode knew Peter's voice, she was so glad she didn't open the gate, but ran in and told Peter to stand outside. " (Acts. 12:13)

The prayer answer knocked on the door - disbelief refused to open

Those attending the prayer meeting said to Rode, "You are from the mind and assembly. But she assured that it was as she said. " (v 15) Unbelief came with the next super-apology. Listen to it: "Those who prayed fervently said: It is his angel."

When they finally opened up and saw him, they were horrified! What a tragic bunch, calling themselves the followers of Christ.

In the end, it was one of the "heartfelt prayers" that opened the door, in a kind of faith. Out there stood the physical Peter, whom the praying gang had only heard, as Rode had. But now it was manifested physically through faith. This was just an unbelieving assembly, the "believing warrior's world" is another.

Unbelief never gets visualized - the faith gets things visualized

The unbeliever never visualizes God's thoughts, speech or words. We clearly see an example of this here. Faith gets visualized God's thoughts, speech, and words.

We see a great example of this here. If we stand firm in the faith, it happens what Peter experienced. I like this: "The gate opened completely by itself." (Acts 12,10)

You see, as we walk God's way and obey God, Satan sees it and he gets respect for you. Gradually, he stays away from you more and more. He knows that Christ lives through you - and then he is beaten every time.

"Everything is possible for the believer. Immediately the child's father cried out, "I believe, help my unbeliever!" "(Mark 9, 23-24) Without the strong, conscious faith, guided by your will, nothing will work for you.

The discovery of "eternity in our hearts (Ecclesiastes 3, 11)"

As I lay on the grass of Sri Lanka before the meeting, I discovered something in Ecclesiastes 3.11: That eternity was embedded in our hearts. This opened a new spiritual understanding. I understood that all people, regardless of religion, have a part of eternity in their hearts. Not in a physical heart, but in the spiritual, central part of a human being. This made my preaching to other religions much easier. Now I knew that part of eternity was in their hearts. When I preached the gospel with that understanding, the response came immediately as spiritual recognition became significant.

 In American Bibles, "the world" stands for "eternity," which I didn't understand - until I discovered that eternity from Hebrew also means the cosmos. Here a brand-new groundbreaking door opened.

A new revelation on the same verse 30 years later

Suddenly I saw that the word "world" was also correct to use. What I saw as a major weakness of the Bible was that no one, neither Norwegian nor English Bibles, had any explanation for this.

You can get the explanation from me here:

From Hebrew, the word "gospel" and the word "world" are from the same basic word, namely "cosmos".

I first saw and understood this from Mark 16, 15 where Jesus gave His final command to the disciples: "Go into all the world (the whole cosmos) and preach the gospel to all creation."
The word "world" here is from Greek and Hebrew and means "cosmos".
The word "eternity" in Ecclesiastes 3, 11 is also from Hebrew and means "cosmos".
This opened a whole new door for my understanding.

The world is what we create around us

The world is what we create around us on earth, out of the spiritual reality within us. Here are two options: You can build your world on earth with God's thoughts and obey Jehovah, or you can build your world on earth with Satan's thoughts and obey them. Every thought comes from the spiritual world. It's all an election campaign. You decide how your world should be. Your world is first and foremost spiritual.

It is manifested physically by your faith and action in boldness on the words of the Bible. We all know this: The battle for the mind has been here since the dawn of time. We are in orders of magnitude such as time, vacuum, space, matter, and energy of scope. We do not have much understanding of this. As rebirths, all eternity (which is spiritual, with certain physical elements in it), is what we are a part of. Most of the cosmos is physically empty for man.

The whole perspective of eternity is our range of motion in the spiritual
We can tear down Satan's fortifications, which are thoughts to our minds, which we again obey. We tear them down by letting God's thoughts, God's written Word, the Bible, prevail instead. The one you obey becomes your Lord. You will

see a bigger picture of your life as a born-again believer in Jesus Christ than before.

My books will constantly be renewed as God guides me further into what I have begun to see here. Everything I come up with is firmly rooted in the written Word of God, the Bible. Welcome to a new world, with new opportunities that you didn't understand were there.

7

How was Jesus' spiritual life?

Jesus did not explain or teach us in any particular way how to relate to the spiritual world. Other than what we can understand about Jesus' work on Calvary and his resurrection from the dead.

I include some Bible sites on the matter, I could have included more, but here is a little to give some revelation on the topic. Now we have already received revelation on the spiritual reality of Jesus' birth and the shepherds in the field. Furthermore, other spiritual realities in the Bible. Now we take a little look at Jesus' own spiritual life, which is not too much about.

Jesus' prayer life and spiritual warfare
Also bring my book with you: Pray through - Praying Faith Prayers.

52

Set aside alone in prayer

"And when he had let the people go, he went up into the mountain to pray; and when evening came, he was there alone.

But the boat was all in the middle of the sea and worked hard against the waves because the wind was against.

But in the fourth watch of the night Jesus came to them, walking on the sea. " (Matt. 14, 23-25)

It is mentioned on some occasions that Jesus was alone in prayer. Here, Jesus had healed the sick and saturated the people with seven loaves and some small fish. Shortly afterwards he went up into the mountains to be in communication and closeness to his Father in heaven. This is where Jesus got his strength to do the task he was sent to do. This was something that Jesus was totally dependent on.

Proximity in silence with the Father

Jesus had no more advantages than other humans. He was the same as all of us. Jesus with his will life, had to make decisions. He had to decide with all his might to gain closeness, knowledge and communication with the Father. He did this in the same way that you and I have to do to get to the position God wants us to be in. This is to work in the supernatural as he would with each one of us.

The kingdom of heaven has come near
Right after Jesus had been in fellowship with God in this event, we see Jesus walking on the water. This shows me in a simple way, what happens when we live in God's presence. Then the heavenly realities are opened to us.

The celestial powers and the earthly reality are drawn closer together
The celestial realities are drawn closer to the physical world, precisely because of your conscious life with, time and tranquility in the presence of God. Where he wants to speak the revealed word to you. The revealed which in turn carries with it the heavenly powers. This is possible for you to get into.
Listen to this verse.

"Jesus says: But if it is by the finger of God that I cast out the evil spirits, then the kingdom of God has come to you." (Luke. 11, 20)

As Jesus brought heaven down, so do you and I.

We see again Jesus was alone in prayer, this time in the Garden of Gethsemane.

Apart from alone in prayer in Gethsemane
"And he tore himself away from them as far as a stone's throw, and fell on his knees and prayed, saying:
Father, if you will, let this lime pass me by!
However, my will not happen but yours!

And an angel from heaven appeared to him and strengthened him.

And he came in fear of death and prayed even more powerfully, and his sweat became like drops of blood, falling to the ground. «
(Luke. 22, 41 - 44)

Here, our Lord and Savior fought His final deci-
sive battle in the spirit, which opened the door
for human salvation.

God revealed himself from heaven through His Son

"Do you not think that I am in the Father and the
Father in me? The words I tell you I do not
speak of myself, but the Father, who abides in
me, he does his deeds.

Believe me that I am in the Father and the Father
in me; if not, believe it anyway for the very sake
of the deeds of faith! " (John. 14, 10-11)

Jesus spoke only the words the Father asked him
to speak, the words that Jesus revealed
Here again we see. It is Jesus' close fellowship
with the Father that made Jesus not speak by
himself, but spoke the revealed words of the Father. He spoke only what the Father asked him to
speak.
Those were the words Jesus had faith to say and
put into action. This is exactly the same way we
can do it.

We always come back to the Hebrew letter that says

"Faith is full certainty of what is hoped for, conviction of things not seen." (Heb, 11, 1)

Here was all of Jesus' secret and here's all of your secret.

8

There must be something more to the prayers

At half past eight in the morning
My wife had stood up. I called out to her in the
kitchen: "I'll stay here and pray for a while". I
had planned how to do this morning. I stood on
my knees and concentrated.

I close for the influence of the senses
Consciously, I said to myself, "I close all the
senses, which take in the impression of the sur-
roundings." I did this to get the opportunity to
receive impressions from the spiritual world.
I said to myself: I put the deeds of the flesh behind me. I did it with the confession that I did.
Why I did, I don't know, but I did (and still do
every time I pray). Then I said, "I open my spiritual life to the world of God, the world of the
Holy Spirit. Let me meet You their Lord ".

The first battle situation you have to win to progress

Then I was completely calm, concentrating on making my thinking life calm down. This is the first spiritual battle situation to be won. Now, after long training, that is no longer the problem. But every now and then, serious work had to be done on this matter.

Believe what you see - you will see it

But I worked on the matter in prayer, thoughts came to me. Behind the thoughts came other thoughts. The other thoughts said, "Believe what you think, it will visualize to you in the spiritual world."

"Is this real?" I thought, "Or is it just something I imagine?" Then came the thought behind the thought again: "Believe what you think, it visualizes itself".

I said stop to all the thoughts of doubt (and other impressions through thoughts) that wanted to keep me from what I was about to experience. It took weeks before I made this work well. It took practice every day, before God. Then one day it got quiet in my mind.

If you manage a second of silence in your mind - you are there

If you manage a second of silence in the mind, you go out into the Spirit with God. For the Lord is a day like a thousand years, and a thousand years as a day. Do you see the perspective? The moment you are silent, God can give you information, which extends over much longer periods of time.

Faith is the key

Close all thoughts out. Refuse to accept any thought, anyway. Accept and believe only God's thoughts.

Just believe

My mind was quiet for a second - and out I disappeared. I saw a faint white light in the distance. I walked out of myself, and disappeared through the white light, into the spiritual world. (The further experiences in the spiritual world I write nothing about, that is not what I want you to grasp in this book first and foremost). What I want is for you to come out into the world of the Spirit yourself and have your own experiences

and get to know the trinity of God in a new,
deeper and totally personal way.

Work on your life

It is not for nothing that the Bible speaks so
clearly about the deeds of the flesh. The deeds of
the flesh are the result of the choices we make
based on the impressions through our senses. It
is our senses that we need to have control over,
these are the ones that give signals into emotions
and thoughts.

We must gain control over everything that will
enter through the senses and open up to everything that God will impart through our feelings
and thoughts from the spiritual side. This is what
you must hold on to and believe - then you are in
the process.

Self-discipline is needed

The deeds of the flesh are not done by prayer,
whatever you think prayer is. Prayer is according
to the Bible's words, communication and closeness to God. Not framing wish lists.

 Hard work with the use of the will needs. This
is a long exercise. Either you give up or you bet.
If you give all you will reach the goal. It is a

flesh that must be disciplined before we get to the point where we enter the world of the Spirit. Paul says something he could not have said if he had not experienced it:

"You foolish Galatians! Who has wronged you, you who have had Jesus Christ painted before your eyes as crucified? " (Gal. 3,1)

Paul probably shared his visualization of Christ for them. Paul had not seen Christ be crucified.

What opened my eye for Spiritual life? (Cosmos, eternity)
It was the necessity of sanctification.

9

Live in victory in the spiritual world

You have no more victory in the spiritual world than you have here in the physical world.
It's no adventure. If you live fundamentally strong in the Lord and His Word, with Jesus Christ as Lord - then you stand just as strong in the spiritual world as in the physical.

The fixed elements of the spirit world
The spirit world in our "atmospheric size" has some fixed elements. Satan's "hiding place", the demon's "hiding place" and the belt of glory of the Holy Spirit, all around the planet. (Joel 3)
Out here, you can be in full victory if you have full victory in your own life on earth.
But it must be arranged first. Targeted training, training and further training are needed.

God's manifest presence - in the spiritual, or here in the physical

God's presence around us and in us makes us different from all other people on earth! In the Garden of Eden, Adam and Eve walked with God until disobedience made them hide in the sight of the Lord God (Genesis 3: 8). At this time man removed himself from the presence of God. The son Cain removed himself even more from the presence of God, as a result of a hardened heart. But God did not give up anyway and continued to long for close fellowship with man whom He loved.

Enoch and Noah

Finally, men like Enoch and Noah came to God, who touched the heart of God with their unshakable quest. As a result, they walked closer to God than anyone else in their millennium after Adam left Eden.

Abraham

Abraham often experienced God's manifest presence throughout life. Such a meeting happened when God came to discuss Sodom and Gomera's future with him. After the judgment on the city, we read, "Early the next morning, Abraham hurried to the place where he had stood before the Lord." (Genesis 19, 27)

This was just one of the many times Abraham enjoyed the fellowship in God's immediate presence.

When Abraham grew old, he said to his servant, "For the Lord, whose presence I have walked in, will send His angel with you and make you successful in your mission." (Genesis 24,40)

Samuel

We read that "Samuel grew up and the Lord was with him, and did not let any of his words fall to the earth." (1 Sam. 3,19)

How could it happen that none of this man's words went wrong? The answer is:

"And the Lord gave Hannah three sons and two daughters. Meanwhile, the boy Samuel grew up with the Lord. " 1 Sam. 2,21)

When we know Him, we say what He says, and our words do not fail.

David
The time in the presence of God, the imperative
David, who loved the presence of God and experienced it as often as anyone in the Old Testament (possibly with the exception of Moses), exclaimed,

 "May Your servant David's house be established in Your presence." (2 Sam. 7:26)

Like Moses, he would not know of any progress that came at the expense of God's presence. Later, when he sinned so badly with adultery and murder, his heartfelt pain was: "Do not cast me away from Your presence, and do not take Your Holy Spirit from me!" (Psalm 51:11) He knew that in truth life would be empty and meaningless outside the presence of God! It was he who wrote the words: "You must show me the way of life. For Your face is the fullness of joy. At Your right hand is eternal joy. (Psalm 16:11)

Psychology says about a person's development from childhood, that the first twelve years of life shape your personality to who you are today. I cannot agree with this. Our genes mean a great deal, a large part of the personality is embedded in us from birth. But certainly not everything.

Listen to what the Scriptures tell us: "Don't go wild, plain company spoils good habits."
(1 Cor. 15,33)

 "He who walks with wise men, becomes wise himself." (Proverbs 13.20)

All the problems were around David for over ten years

What about David? He was alone in the wilderness when "all who were in need, all who were in debt, and all who were bitter in the soul, gathered around him. This is how he became the leader for them. There were about 400 men with him. " (1 Sam. 22,2) For a bunch to spend over ten years with! The dissatisfied, the troubled and the debt slaves!
They were angry, nervous, and most likely unruly and insensitive.

Did they shape David's personality?
No. Why not? Because David spent a lot of time in God's presence! He maintained a princely attitude. He chose to let God shape himself - and not circumstances!

He "did not go in a strange yoke with disbelief."
(2 Cor. 6:14)

The result was that those who were with David for over ten years were shaped into great leaders who became famous for many generations! Hear this wonderful verse:

"My Heart Heard You Say: Come Talk to Me."
And my heart replies, "Lord, I come."
(Psalm 27: 8)

The presence of God shaped David
This was David's life, he spent so much time with the Lord that he not only affected 400 weeping men but influenced an entire nation! He was an influencer, because he spent time with the source of wisdom, all knowledge and all understanding.

David did not do it to get God's wisdom - he pressed in because he longed for God's heart, to come as close to God as possible. He loved Him more than anything else, and the reason was that he spent so much time with Him. The more time he spent with the Lord, the more he loved the Lord.

Solomon

If only David's son, Solomon, had inherited the burning longing. He saw the God of Israel twice, and possessed greater wisdom than anyone before and after him. But he did not realize the importance of staying in God's presence. At the end of his life, when the years were spent, he wrote the sad book of Ecclesiastes / Preachers. Despite owning wisdom, unbelievable wealth, and the most beautiful women on earth. Despite fame and influence both far and near, he had nothing else to say but: "Everything is emptiness and the pursuit of wind!" If he had had his father David's heart, Israel's history would have been quite different. We could go on through the Old Testament, look at several similar examples, but I think these are enough.

1 0

You need to work on this
to get it in place

I want you to see the seriousness of the serious, conscious relationship you have to work and train and get into place. This is a meticulous work that you must not give up before you have it. Once in place, make sure you stay there. This is the hardest and most important work you will ever do in your life. As I said before: You have no more victory in the spiritual world than you have here in the physical. We must stand equally strong in both dimensions, the third and the fourth - the physical world and the spiritual world.

The fruits of the Spirit are what we need in our lives

You have to take hold of your life, then any positive change you need happens. It is the rendering of the flesh, and the covering of the fruits of the Spirit, that is needed. What you have, you can give to others - if they want it. (Gal 5: 16-22)

A Life Near God:
We must live in victory in the physical world and in the spiritual world - the key is a life in the presence of God!

Glory is in the presence of God
How could Isaiah, Ezekiel, and the apostle John see the glory of the Lord and survive so that they could write about it? The answer is simple: They were in the spiritual, and out of the body. Mortal bodies cannot stand in the presence of the Holy Lord in all His glory. He is the consuming fire in which there is no darkness.
(Heb. 12:29; 1 John. 1,5)

Paul writes about Jesus:
"He who is the blessed and the only powerful, the King of kings and Lord of lords. He alone has immortality and lives in a light no one can approach. He who no human has seen or can see. " (1Tim. 6,15.16)

Jesus lives in a light that cannot be approached and that no human being can see or have seen. The psalmist even states that the Lord has shone on Him like a cloak. (Psalm 104.2)

It was easy for Paul to write this because he had experienced a measure of this unattainable light from His glorious presence on the road to Damascus. He rendered it to King Agrippa in this way:

"At noon while I was on my way, King, I saw a light from heaven. It was brighter than the sun and shone around me and those traveling with me. " (Acts 26:13)

Paul did not see Jesus' face, he only saw the light from Him. And it overwhelmed and overshadowed the light of the bright sun in the Middle East! Paul was in the presence of the glory of God.

What is the glory of the Lord?
If we read what Moses asked of God: He not only asked for God's presence, he went further, he asked to see His glory.

Moses said, "I pray You, show me Your glory!" (Exodus 33:18)

The Hebrew word for glory is "kabowd". Strong's Bible Handbook defines it as "the weight of something, but only figuratively, in a good sense." The definition also speaks of splendor, opulence and honor. Moses asked God to show Himself in all His splendor. " Take a close look at God's answer:

"I will let My goodness pass over your face, and I will proclaim the name of the Lord to you.» (Ex. 33:19)

Moses prayed for all His glory, and God answered with "all My goodness." The Hebrew word for goodness is "twwb". It means goodness in the broadest form of the word. In other words, without holding anything back.

Before an earthly king enters his throne hall, his name is proclaimed by a herald. The proclamation is followed by trumpet fanfare as he enters the throne hall in all his glory. The greatness of the king is revealed, and at his court there is no doubt who is king.

His majestic presence fills everyone with awe. But what if this same monarch was strolling around the streets of his city, dressed in plain clothes, without any servants? The truth is, what was clear in the court context would be lost outside the castle - because many who passed him would not recognize him. His presence would not be as impressive and noticeable as in the throne room, where he was in all his glory. Basically, this is exactly what God did for Moses by saying, "I will proclaim My name and pass you by in all My glory."

In the New Testament, we hear that "the glory of the Lord is revealed in the face / face of Jesus Christ." (2 Cor 4: 6)

Many who have been in the presence of the Lord have testified that they saw Jesus in a vision and looked into His face. It is very possible, but I can promise you that they did not see all His glory. It is important to have a clear understanding of when to move into the presence of God.

A mental relationship with God is mechanical and devoid of spirit

To say that one understands and knows a great deal about the gospel truths is one thing.

The price to pay for living in the presence of God is another thing and are the reality

Another thing, which is reality, is to live in the spiritual dimension always. We can do that once we have decided on it and pay the price it costs to get there. A mental relationship with God is mechanical and devoid of spirit. We were made to stay in Him, in reality, not just in theory. We should never be satisfied until we experience this in its fullness. Jesus died to remove the curtain that separated us from the very presence of God. This is why the psalmist calls it out:

"How glorious and lovable Your dwellings are (there You rest), Lord, the God of armies. My soul longs, yes, to be consumed with longing for the Lord's courts. My heart and my flesh cry out and sing with joy and joy to the living God. Even the sparrow has found a home, and the swallow has found a nest where she can lay her cubs, your altars, the Lord of hosts, my King and

God. Blessed and blessed (happy, lucky, envious) are those who live in Your house and dwell in Your presence; they must sing Your praise and promise You, all day long. Selah."
(Psalm 84: 2-5)

11

The evolution of faith in the physical world and in the Spirit in the world of spirits

What is Reality?

There are many different impressions people get from an event. We can only look at that testimony in a trial. The same event is seen in different ways by different people. Another closer reality for you, is perhaps what impression you have of life? Dictionaries' definition of reality is: "... what is real, an actual thing, situation or event." According to the objective analysis, this is the reality.

Reality is objective and subjective

But reality is not only objective, it also has a subjective or personal side, rooted in what one feels, believes or believes. If we see it in this perspective, the reality is like this: "It will be as you thought." (Matt. 8:13)

Unreal - really

In this personal perspective, what is really for one human being often becomes unreal for that other human being. I have traveled extensively in Asia and have stayed many times in private. Their home can often just be a ground floor bamboo hut. There they lie and sleep on thin mats. In Norway we have designer villas, of the highest quality in everything. The beds are like a dream, almost like sleeping on a suitably soft cloud. Although these two realities are totally different, both are equally real and subjectively real for each of us.

Let's learn a principle from this example

Whatever a group of people agree to create through connectivity, compromise and continuous use will ultimately define reality for them. Do you recognize yourself here? It is very important to understand this, because when we agree with the standards and principles of the Kingdom of God, our entire definition of society will change.

A biblical example of this

"Look, they are one people, and they all share
the same language. This is the first thing they do.
Now, nothing will be impossible for them, whatever they think of doing." (Genesis 11: 6)

Whatever they may think they can do, they can
do - nothing is impossible for them
This the Lord himself said of the wicked Baby-
lonians. He said that no matter what they intend
to do, they have the resources to do it.

Do you doubt the validity of this statement?

Would you be among those who suspected and
apologized to those who imagined that they were
on the moon? You might have been among those
making fun of the idea that voices and images
could be disseminated across the globe using invisible waves? You might have ridiculed the idea
of a weapon so powerful that it could destroy all
life on earth?

"Creating reality"

**Man cannot create, but we cooperate with the
Creator.**

These things are still part of our reality today, thanks to people with the ability to "create reality". Some of us humans have a greater wealth of opportunities to realize than others. If a person's mind can imagine something, and they can make others believe it, their spirit can do it. And with few exceptions, nothing will be impossible, even for such a small group as two or three, if they just accept and believe that something can happen. It is precisely this day's war in the congregation that concentrates. The devil wants us to accept Christianity as it is, as if divisiveness, sin, and spiritual powerlessness are all God has arranged for the believers on earth. Satan wants us to agree, thus supporting this distorted image of the church / community.

We must agree with God's plan

The Plan for a Holy, Undivided, Powerful Church: The Lord has called us to establish His kingdom, not to remain in the place of rest. He wants us to take the territory, establish the kingdom of God and preach the gospel according to Mark 16: 15-20. We build a strong personal relationship with the personalities of Father, Son, Jesus Christ and the Holy Spirit in the spiritual world. At the same time, we proclaim the gospel to the last unreached peoples to promote Jesus' return.

We serve in the physical and spiritual world simultaneously

We do this in the physical world. The practical exercise of Mark 16:15 in the physical, in faith, and the victories we gain in the physical, occur in parallel in the spiritual world, out there in the cosmos somewhere. It happens out there in the spiritual dimension. Not in the cosmic / physical dimension similar to the one we have here on earth.

1 2

How Do We Grow Spiritually?
What is the meaning
of a Spiritual life?

Let's look at the little that is revealed about Jesus' spiritual life, which will be a role model for our spiritual life.
A life of sanctification that we have already taken up is an absolute necessity, in order to live / be life in this reality.

The kingdom of God
"Jesus said, But if it is by the finger of God that I cast out the evil spirits, then the kingdom of God has come to you." (Luke. 11, 20)

We see the same thing again in Matt. gospel:
"Jesus said, but if it is by the Spirit of God that I cast out the evil spirits, then the kingdom of God has come to you." (Matt. 12:28)

Jesus' conscious faith

This is not to be misunderstood. The kingdom of God was always where Jesus was. It was a reality and a conscious presence in Jesus. In the spiritual and spiritual life of Jesus. It was God's Kingdom Jesus deliberately used in the physical world. Jesus' faith in the kingdom of God in him, and through him to the physical world, was a belief with the full certainty (Heb. 11, 1).

"Jesus said, And this gospel of the kingdom shall be preached throughout the whole earth for a witness (martyrdom) for all peoples, and then shall the end come." (Matt. 24:14)

Here Jesus says straight out. The Kingdom of Heaven will be in us, where we are, as Jesus' disciples.

"Then we are messengers, ambassadors, in Jesus' place." (2 Cor. 5, 20)

With the Kingdom of God in us, through us, to the world around us.

The Kingdom of God must be consciously sought if it is to become a conscious reality through us

"And when Jesus had let the people go, he went up into the mountain to pray; and when evening came, he was there alone. " (Matt. 14,23)

The necessary communication with the Kingdom of God at all times.

Just before Jesus went up the mountain to pray, he had healed the sick and saturated about five thousand men, besides women and children. He had saturated these with five loaves and two fish. After being on the mountain and praying, he went on the water and when he came ashore, he healed the sick. Read chapter 14 of Matthew's gospel.

Communication with God leads to results

Is prayer the way we have always thought it is? "Prayer is an art that only the Holy Spirit can teach us." (Spurgeon)

Prayer has been somewhat abstract for most Christians. It has been difficult to get a grasp on how to do it. There have been several types of "ritual prayers" in various Christian contexts.

"For it is sanctified by the Word and prayer of God." (1 Tim. 4, 5)

"But the copper altar I want to keep praying." (2 King 16, 15)

The importance of repentance

This is where the importance of repentance comes in with prayer. Repentance must be done if prayer is to come forth. If our prayers are to reach into the spiritual and meet God.

In the Old Testament worship, sacrifice and purification of the sins of the people were kept in the tabernacle. The copper altar in the courtyard of the tabernacle was the most important. It was sin and the atonement altar. The copper stands for something solid.

But what is prayer?

I offer some simple explanations from Hebrew on what prayer is:

"Entevxis" (Hebrew)

This word means "meeting, meeting and conversation". This tells me that these are talking about personalities that hold intelligent conversations. That is to say we should have conversation with God.

"Baqar" (Hebrew)

This word means "look after, care for, look for". This tells me that there is a caring love in prayer.

"Daras" (Hebrew)

Means "follow, seek, worship, tread, visit, frequent, ask". Here, I see prayer means seeking God until we find Him, further building up personal relationships with God, the Creator of God, the God who is our Lord as we worship.

(There are several words to include from the basic language. But I think these meanings are the most explanatory of what prayer is).

Personal direct contact with God the Father

That is how Jesus sought his father in solitude and got the contact and again the power he needed at all times. Similarly, it will be for you, as a born-again Christian.

The toughest prayer fight Jesus had was in Gethsemane's garden. The spiritual struggle can never become a reality in our lives until we have done what is necessary in our carnal, physical life and let the word of God prevail. God's Word must be given voluntarily by us in control. We must voluntarily allow our senses to submit to the Word of God in us.

This is the spiritual struggle of the "prayer" in the way described from Hebrew.

The bean fight, is an election campaign

What do you choose to control, God's thoughts to you in words or Satan's thoughts to you in words, Your will determines the outcome of the battle. Now we do not want to face the battle Jesus faced in Gethsemane, but we still take a little look at it.

"And Jesus got rid of them and got down on his knees and prayed and said:

The necessity of your own will
Father! If you will, let this lime pass me by! However, do not happen my will, but yours!

The closeness of the physical and God Spiritual world to one another

And an angel from heaven appeared to him and strengthened him.

And he came in fear of death and prayed even more fiercely, and his sweat became like drops of blood, falling to the ground. "
(Luke. 22. 41 - 44)

Here we see the kingdom of God, the world of the Spirit of God came to Jesus with an angel who strengthened Jesus. Here we see the presence of the Kingdom of God. Jesus was in the position where the powers of the Kingdom of God, the powers of the Spiritual world, cooperated with the surrendered life of Jesus to His Father.

When you choose God's way - always
When your will is determined to always choose
God's way, the powers of the Kingdom of God,
the powers of God's Spiritual world, will be with
you, as they were with Jesus.
Then this verse will become a reality in you.

"Jesus said to the disciples: Do you not believe
that I am in the Father and the Father in me? The
words I say to you I do not speak of myself, but
the Father, who abides in me, he does his deeds.
" (John. 14:10)

Listen further.

"Jesus saith unto the disciples, But the Com-
forter of the Holy Ghost, whom the Father shall
send in the name of the receiving, he shall teach
you all things, and remind you of all things
which I have spoken unto you." (John. 14:26)

Jesus says to the disciples:

"If you stay in me and my words stay in you, ask
for what you want and you will get it.
(John. 15: 7)

When God's Word lives in you, God lives in you by His Spirit in you. When you live your life surrendered to God and you seek Him, He will speak to you. His speech to you is always God's revelation to you. Everything God reveals to you, you think. What you think you can put into practice in the physical, earthly.
I mention this Bible site again

"Jesus said to the disciples: Do you not believe that I am in the Father and the Father in me? The words I say to you I do not speak of myself, but the Father, who abides in me, he does his deeds. " (John. 14:10)

Now you get revelation about this. Take it and start living it out.

"And when you pray, do not frame many words like the heathen; for they believe that they are heard when they use many words.

Therefore, don't act like them! for your father knows what you need before you ask him.
"(Matt. 6, 7 - 8)
Listen, listen and do.

War in the sky (our atmosphere)

"Then war broke out in heaven: Michael and his angels went to war against the dragon. The dragon fought with his angels, but was overcome, and they could no longer find space for them in heaven. " (Rev. 12.7-89)

This event is not easy for us to understand. How do angels and demons wage war? Creatures that do not die of wounds - how and with what do they fight? How do they defeat each other? Without going beyond our boundaries of knowledge, we can safely say this: All warfare in the spiritual center is an important question: Who is to control reality on earth? Heaven or perdition?

Power - the unity between people and the spirit world
When it comes to the war between angels and demons, the fight does not depend on physical

weapons. It depends on the power - unity that exists between humanity and the spirit world.

We read in Ephesians that "powers and authorities" possess "heaven." (Eph. 6:12)

And we read that it is the Father's expressed will to summarize all things in Christ, "everything in heaven and on earth." (Eph. 1,10)

Here, God's wonderful plan is revealed: He intends through Ecclesia (the elect, those gathered in the squares, the community, the congregation) to proclaim His diverse wisdom "to the powers and authorities of the heavens." (Eph. 3.10)

When the body of Christ on earth agrees with his head in heaven, the powers of darkness in the heavens are banished by Christ's own Spirit.

When Christ's fellowship on earth is aggressive, ongoing
In other words, when the body of Christ on earth is ongoing in its unity with the will and word of God - into the spiritual, into the soul, and into

the physical - God's presence in the spiritual world increases and is released. The influence of Satan and the forces of darkness on earth is displaced proportionally. Soon after, this is manifested in the physical world, the human world. We will see revival, healing, miracles, human salvation and the gospel reach out to all unreached peoples of the world.

When the church (ecclesia) is passive
Indifferent or carnal, the powers of the abyss extend their dominion over the actions of mankind. Marriage is growing, crime is rising, the release unit is running fast. We must understand that our relationship, our understanding, our prayer, our fellowship, and our unity with God are absolutely necessary for the accomplishment of God's plan on earth!

The spiritual world Satan works in
"When he speaks lies, Satan, he speaks of his own, for he is a liar and the father of lies."
(John 8,44)

Here we see clearly Scripture reveals Satan as the father of lies. His sphere of activity is the spirit world that in "time" surrounds and covers the consciousness of mankind. This area clearly calls the Bible the "heaven". (Eph 6:12) From this spirit, Satan works.

In the heavenlies
When I mentioned his hiding place in the first chapter, he has the "hiding place" here in the sky. Satan's pursuit extends throughout the sky, into the entire cosmos. Here Satan works to control and corrupt the human mind, through the illusions of thought created by the lusts and fears of the flesh. Thoughts sent as arrows from Satan. The power of lies is not only to speak falsehoods, nor is this world an illusion. The lie of the enemy seems to have the greatest power when people think that this world, as it is, is the only world we can live in! The truth is that God is in the process of establishing His kingdom, and that all realities will eventually submit to and be governed by this kingdom!
(Heb. 12,26-28 Rev. 11:15)

Here, then, there is no talk of heaven coming here on this earth. On the other hand, the glory and power of heaven is unlimited available to us here in time.

We are ambassadors of heaven, with the message of salvation to the entire creature. The glory of heaven is demonstrated in the earth through the servants of God.

In the future sometime, all the saints will travel to the Eternal City and the Kingdom of Heaven. The struggle is not only in our near-to-earth spiritual atmosphere, but in the entire cosmos. The struggle extends completely to everything God has created.

15

Our weapons

The weapon God has given us to fight the lies of the enemy is God's Word, the Bible, "the sword of the Spirit." (Eph. 6.17)

Jesus said it so significally: His Word "they are Spirit and life". (Jn 6,63)

It means that the content, the meaning of the written Word of God, represents an actual reality. It is then the living Spirit of the Kingdom of God. It is the Spirit that can create.

"God spoke and it happened, He commanded and it stood there." (Psalm 33.9)

The word Jehovah from Hebrew means: The everlasting existence that reveals Himself. Do you see God's nature, God's personality in His name? He is everything! He is the creative and the only one who can create. He is life!

In the Greek language, "truth" and "reality" are the same

We must also understand that the Greek language, on which the New Testament is written, had no specific word for "reality." For them, "truth" and "reality" were the same! When we think of the "Spirit of truth," we must also include the concept of "reality" in our understanding. It means that the Holy Spirit and the Word of God are the very reality!

This point is absolutely necessary to be clear

This must be understood. In our war on who is to control the world of men, the Word of God, which receives power from His Spirit, the only weapon of the Church of Christ (the reborn), has been distributed. The living Word of the Spirit is the Truth.

Paul taught us that spiritual warfare is especially about "tearing down fortifications." But what are these fortifications? They are the lies Satan has embedded in our thought patterns, and which remain "reality" to us as we accept and believe in them.

We do not often fall into sin because we are deceived. Every sin is obscured by a certain amount of lies and deception. But when the lie is uncovered and destroyed, by freeing our thought processes from illusions - we will discover that the purity, perfection and truth of Jesus in us gives us the eternal hope of glory.

"For whom God would make known how rich in glory this secret is among the Gentiles, it is Christ among you, the hope of glory."
(Col. 1.27)

God is the Word
"In the beginning was the Word, and the Word was with God, and the Word was God."
(John. 1,1)

Christ is the Word
"And the Word became flesh, and dwelt among us, and we beheld the glory of Christ - a glory which the only begotten Son hath of his Father - full of grace and truth." (John.1,14)

The Holy Spirit is the Word

"For they are three that bear witness:
The spirit, the water, and the blood, and these
three go out into one." (1 John 5: 7.8)

Sacrifices of the Old Testament
shows that the blood of listless, flawless animals
was sprinkled on the scroll. Why?
Because the book is lifeless for anyone who
reads it, unless the blood has been there beforehand! In the same way it is today. The Bible is
lifeless for us unless the blood has been with us
beforehand.

Those born again have the opportunity to understand the Bible, no one else
Only one type of people has the opportunity to
gain insight into the Word, those who are born
again, purified in the blood, and who live in the
covenant. This is our part in Christ. We can only
rest in the covenant, rest in the blood. We don't
have to do anything ourselves. God sent His own
Son, His own blood.

"And they have triumphed over him by the blood of the Lamb, and the words which they testified." (Rev.12,11)

The testimony, the proclamation of God's Word on the basis of the Word - with the full knowledge and conviction that it lasts forever! The blood sacrifices in the Old Testament only showed us weakly the meaning of Jesus' blood, and what authority it is in the name of Jesus. The blood is shed once and for all. We can go straight into the sanctuary - on the grounds of blood.

"Therefore, when we brethren, in the blood of Jesus, have the boldness to enter into the sanctuary, let us come forth with sincere hearts, in the full certainty of faith, purified on the hearts." (Heb. 10:19)

Our perfect victory
Our victory is in the Word of God, the Word of the Bible.
Our victory is in the Atonement of Jesus Christ on Calvary.
Our victory is in the precious blood of Jesus.

Our victory is in the Holy Spirit, God Jehovah is the Holy One. He is the Holy Spirit.

Stand on the Word of God

As I have always preached, and that is the foundation of the strong Christian life: It is the solid foundation of God's Word. It has to be purposefully built into it, from day one after rebirth. It all starts with you as a natural human being: You are born again. A new life in God's quality has come into you. Now the work begins to grow in the spiritual life, in the Holy Spirit, in you. Here it must be built solid, strong and with quality. When this is in place, the time has come to "seek further into the world of the Spirit," in the Holy Spirit.

"He spoke and it happened, He commanded, and it stood there." (Psalm 33.9)

Here we see God speaking, as He also did when He said:

"Get light! And it became light. " (Genesis 1,3)

Here we see God speaking words. God's Word is creative. What creates is the energy of the Spirit of God, if I may call it that. If we take a look at Genesis 2.5, we see something enlightening:

The Word, the Spirit and the man – the man a physical realization of the Word

The revelation that came under the toothbrush

I remember back in 1979, I was to speak in a Methodist church in Norway. A few days in advance, something started to challenge me. I saw the creation in the first two chapters of Genesis. In the first chapter everything was spoken to life and in the last verse of the chapter God saw that everything was very good.

"God saw everything He had done, see, it was very good." (Genesis 1:32)
Then I proceeded to chapter 2.5. It said: "There was no bush in the ground yet."

Now I didn't understand anything. I said to the Lord: You must reveal this to me. The next day God revealed it to me as I stood brushing my teeth in the morning. In Chapter 1, He showed me that here was the Word of God spoken, just as we have the written Word of God, the Bible today.

The written Word of God alone was not enough

In chapter 2.5 God showed me that the written / spoken Word of God alone was not enough. The written Word of God had to be made alive (revealed) by the Holy Spirit, the Spirit of God. Verse 5 tells me it "had not rained on earth yet."

Then a new light, a new revelation came to me: The water was a picture of the Holy Spirit. Now I understood, the Holy Spirit had to make the words come alive. It was in this way that the "dead" words could become the living Word of God. This was not enough, it also had to be a human instrument through which the living Word of God could work through. The Bible says in the same chapter verse 7: "There was no man to cultivate the earth."

Now that man had come, all necessary elements were present: The Word, the Holy Spirit, and man. From verses 8-14 we see all things being created physically and coming into place. Here we see clearly that from the beginning God uses the same method of creating things that Jesus taught us in the gospels to get things create**d.**

Hear what Jesus said: The revelation that came under the toothbrush

I remember back in 1979, I was to speak in a Methodist church in Norway. A few days in advance, something started to challenge me. I saw the creation in the first two chapters of Genesis. In the first chapter everything was spoken to life and in the last verse of the chapter God saw that everything was very good.

"God saw everything He had done, see, it was very good." (Genesis 1:32)
Then I proceeded to chapter 2.5. It said: "There was no bush in the ground yet."

Now I didn't understand anything. I said to the Lord: You must reveal this to me. The next day God revealed it to me as I stood brushing my teeth in the morning. In Chapter 1, He showed me that here was the Word of God spoken, just as we have the written Word of God, the Bible today.

The written Word of God alone was not enough
In chapter 2.5 God showed me that the written / spoken Word of God alone was not enough.
The written Word of God had to be made alive (revealed) by the Holy Spirit, the Spirit of God.
Verse 5 tells me it "had not rained on earth yet."

Then a new light, a new revelation came to me: The water was a picture of the Holy Spirit. Now I understood, the Holy Spirit had to make the words come alive. It was in this way that the "dead" words could become the living Word of God. This was not enough, it also had to be a human instrument through which the living Word of God could work through. The Bible says in the same chapter verse 7: "There was no man to cultivate the earth."

Now that man had come, all necessary elements were present:
the Word, the Holy Spirit, and man.

From verses 8-14 we see all things being created physically and coming into place. Here we see clearly that from the beginning God uses the same method of creating things that Jesus taught us in the gospels to get things created. Hear what Jesus said:

"It is the Spirit that makes alive, the flesh helps nothing. The words that I have spoken to you are spirit and are life. " (John. 6.63)

"Jesus further said: Everything is possible for the believer." (Mark. 9,23)

The word faith is a verb

All verbs are words of action. So, what does Scripture say? Take God's Word - act on it - and the Holy Spirit lets it happen! Do you see the potential for a strong life in the power of the Holy Spirit when Jesus is Lord in your life - and you live surrendered to Him…

Faith increases

I did this more or less consciously from the time I was born again: Filled with the written Word of God. It made my trust and faith in the Bible and Christ great, and it just got stronger and stronger.

The Bible proved itself

As early as the first few months as a Christian, I experienced that people were healed and set free when I prayed for them. The basis for that was precisely my bold confidence and faith in the Word of the Bible and Christ Jesus. Our lives should be channels of revelation for the realities of God.

16

World evangelism was underway

It took over two years - and I was in the process of world evangelism. It became my main task for the Lord. I was in East Africa on my first overseas trip. The Lord was there. Likewise, the accompanying signs and miracles. Humans were saved in large numbers, and many were healed and set free from demons. I already had an unshakable faith in the Lord's Word, but my wisdom might be questioned. It needed, and needs all of its life through, constant improvement.

A human birth and growth

One thing is to be born; another thing is to grow. Every birth is "free" for the person born as a natural human being, but then with a kind of unconscious will (which is anything but a reflex), from the first day, the food that is presented is swallowed. If you do not eat, it will not be long before you are dead. If you eat, you grow. If you train on top of it all to get healthy food, you become stronger. The natural birth works exactly like the spiritual one. Only in another dimension, under other laws.

No unconscious will in the spiritual
There is a difference and it is that in the spiritual life no unconscious will or reflex works. Here must life in from day one. You must want to eat your food, that is, the Word of God - and obey the Word, to grow spiritually.

"For our weapons are not for men, but they have their power from God, and can cast their fort into gravel. We tear down thought buildings and everything big and proud that rises against the knowledge of God, and we capture every thought under obedience to Christ. "
(2 Cor. 10: 4-5)

"But everything that is revealed by the light comes for the day, and everything that comes for the day becomes light." (Eph. 5, 8-13)

When you confess your sins, they become light. They are no longer in the dark, they are no longer secrets.
When the light is turned on in a dark room, the darkness becomes light.

"If we confess our sins, He is faithful and righteous, so He forgives us our sins and cleanses us from all injustice." (1 John 1.9)

Again, it is a matter of confessing the sins. God is faithful and righteous, so He forgives and cleanses you from all sin and injustice.

"But thank God, who in Christ always leads us in His victory and through us spreads the knowledge of Him as a scent, in every place."
(2 Cor. 2:14)

It is victory here and now, if we allow Christ to live in us, through His Word, the Bible.

"For God gave us not the spirit of discouragement, but power, love, and the spirit of sincerity." (2 Tim. 1,7)

Do not fear, which is a threat to Satan. Always remember that Satan is "the father of lies, there is no truth in him".

"Thus, at His death, He would put an end to him who reigned in death, that is, the devil, and deliver all those who, for fear of death, were in bondage all his life." (Heb. 2,14.15)

Satan will always try to make you believe that he has power over you. But if you live by eating the Word of God, then you know that the Bible says, "Christ has put an end to him who reigned over us." Use the name of Jesus and the written Word of God and break the power of Satan's lies.

"And we know that all things serve the good of God, whom He has called for His free will." (Rom. 8, 28.29)

If God allows all things to benefit you when you love Him, there can never be any harm with you. God has chosen you in advance to be likened to the image of His Son.

"Yes, I have given you power to tread on snakes and scorpions and given you power over all the enemy's power, and nothing will harm you."
(Luke. 10.19)

"It was to put an end to the deeds of the enemy that the Son of God revealed Himself."
(1 John. 3,8)

Believe yourself free
You are free, not because you feel free – but because you believe in freedom. Every time you express your faith, you create freedom as a true reality. You trust that as you pray, God's army of angels stand in your back. God's army is many times bigger, and more victorious than Satan's army. The most important thing in this context is that Christ Jesus won a perfect victory over Satan and the demons – once, for all eternity – on the cross at Calvary. All this stands with you against evil. Together with Jesus it cannot fail.

"Therefore, submit to God, resist the devil and he will flee from you."
(James 4.7) (Also read Isaiah 53 and 54,11-17 and 2 King 6, 15-18)

Victory is ours in Jesus name, if the foundation is laid right. This foundation of your spiritual awareness and growth must be in place before you enter the spiritual world.

It's victory!

17

On the way into the depths

Are you ready?
You must first make sure that you live in full victory, in your own life. If you do, you know it. The victory you carry in you is the victory you are able to bring out, to help others. You have to know, which is a step further than believing. You must live in the realm of conviction with your faith in Christ Jesus and His Atonement at Calvary. There must not be a shadow of doubt in your spiritual existence regarding these things. You must know, without a doubt, that the victory Christ Jesus won was for you personally and all other human beings born and living or living on planet Earth (Tellus).

Then when Jesus knew that everything was accomplished for the Scriptures to be fulfilled, He says, "I thirst." There was a tub full of vinegar. They then put a sponge full of vinegar on an ice cream stand and held it up to His mouth. When Jesus had received the vinegar, He said, "It is finished." And He bowed His head and gave up the spirit. (19.28 to 30)

You are the giant in the spirit, with a foundation unshakable in the Atonement, which goes into the spirit, wars and wins the war.

"For all that is born of God overcomes the world, and this is the victory that overcometh the world; our faith. " (John. 5,4)

You never have more victory outward than you have inward. The victory you live daily in your own life is the victory you are able to exert to other people. Nothing more than that. If you live in this, then you are ready.

Preparation

You need to check yourself out if everything in your life is in the light. Go before the Lord and check your conscience. See that everything is fine.

If you have some Satan's snare on you, you are not ready for a task like this. Then the demons will see the opportunity to jump on you too. If you have all things in the light, ask Jesus' blood for protection. Let the shield of Christ's blood cover you.

The Bible says, "And they have triumphed over him, Satan by the blood of the Lamb, and the word they testified, and they had not loved their lives, even unto death." (Rev. 12,11)

Christ, with His own blood, won eternal redemption and Satan was forever a defeated enemy. The precious, pure blood of Jesus Christ is testified in the mercy seat of heaven as the eternal covenant blood, with an eternally defeated Satan in the lake of fire - forever.

"And not with the blood of goats and calves, but with His own blood, once entered into the sanctuary, and won an eternal redemption." (Heb 9, 2) Without blood being shed, no forgiveness occurs. Verse 22:

And almost everything is cleansed with blood according to the law, and without blood being shed, forgiveness does not happen. "

If you are here now, Satan knows you and you know him. Preparations are done. You are the giant who goes into the deep, in humility, but with authority in the name of Jesus.

"All that is born of God overcomes the world, and this is the victory that has overcome the world, our faith." (1 John. 5,4)

Go forward

As you now advance toward Satan, you never stop. If you stop, he'll start to slide, and you can then be tilted back to setback in the fight. Go ahead all the time. When you oppose, then go against - and through to victory. Keep the victory in mind. Our victory was won 2,000 years ago, but Satan has wrongfully taken our territories because we have not claimed our rights in Christ. Now it is over, we are not giving Satan space.

"Do not give Satan space." (Eph. 4.27)

What you are now doing is demanding your right, simple and fine. But Satan has held this our right undisturbed for so long. And he has seen so many weak Christians that he has not cared about.

When a giant like you comes, he is not used to such things, he has only seen weak Christians. He thinks you are easily matched but gets shocked when he sees you.

You are moving forward - and are not going to stop. Satan knows he has "trouble". Remember: People around you are Satan's first choice of tools to break you. Be careful who you have around you. Have only the "believing giants" around you. Those who can lift you, do not push you down.

In your payroll alone.

I recommend you go into your payroll alone. You must obtain and understand your position and place in the spirit. This may take time. Remember you are the giant of Christ Jesus. Bend your knees and close your eyes. (Or another position that is comfortable for you).

The payroll, your personal sanctuary.

When you walk into your secret chamber alone, this is your personal sanctuary, your personal arena, where you have gone aside with God.

God is spirit and you must have contact with Him in the spiritual world.

This is where in the spiritual world Satan moves too, so this is where we meet him and his demons. This is where you learn to understand Satan's way of working. You can reveal him and defeat him.

Make sure your payroll is free of distracting sound and visual impressions, yes, all things that will appeal to your senses.

Close the shutters to the windows of the senses and open the shutters inward in the spirit. Now there is no outside impression that we should concentrate on. Now, one and only is the spiritual world.

We seek the greatest possible contact with it to carry out our assignments. It is also here in the spirit that we develop our most intimate relationship with God. Here in the spirit there are several arenas you will get to know.

Concentrate on the work of calming down your soul

Now you have to want your life in full. The first thing you do is lift all the deeds of the meat out at a distance. You see it out there, you have control over it.

You put your soul / personality under the control of your will. If you control this, you live in victory over the meat.

No room for the flesh

If it turns out that you have problems in areas of your flesh, then it must be completely arranged and obtained victory - and survived in victory over. Do it before trying on what we are currently doing. You will not enter into any of this without victory in your own life. On the other hand, you will be winking at the demons. There is even more trouble than you have had so far.

But if the victory in your life is clear, then you move on.

Under the authority of the Lord

Now you consciously leave your will under the authority of the Lord - and you are beginning to get disciplined and calmed down your personality / soul. This is 100% necessary.

Satan will do everything he can to upset you. He doesn't want you to win the victory here, so you can move on into the spirit. Remember, we live in a spiritual world first and foremost.

The spiritual battle is underway

The devil tries to knock you out at startup. Can you see what I'm talking about? I know you do. All spiritual attacks come through our emotions and thoughts, with desires and other disturbing thoughts. This is the only way the devil can contact you, disturb you. Satan will attack you in your life, through emotions and thoughts. Everything in your life is stored on your personal hard drive, in your soul / personality. Here Satan is fishing. Therefore, all sensory impressions to you must be stopped. With your life of will you have to calm down everything you can of emotions and thoughts.

Thoughts and feelings always go against each other. What you feel, you think. What you think you feel.

Satan does not want you to go into the depths of the spirit.
This must be clear to you. Here you will win your victories - in depth.
Once the victory is won here in the personality / soul arena, you are ready to move on. The mental (personality) struggle can last a long time. Are you ready for this? Or will you give up before you get started? It may take time before you are ready for the depth. Not many are willing to do this. Fasting can be a help here. Feel free to fast throughout the prayer process.

Paul: "But I say, walk in the Spirit, and do not make the lusts of the flesh. For the flesh lusts against the Spirit and the Spirit against the flesh. They oppose each other so you don't do what you want. " (Gal. 5,16.17)

There are always some things, which don't even have to be that big. Small or large in the meat, it is an obstacle approach. Now everything is betting on the victory!

Why fast?
Well, for one purpose: You get a greater concentration on the spiritual things,
than the concentration on the physical things.
You become much clearer in the soul
and the spiritual. This is the sole purpose of fasting.

"But show us in all things as the servants of God, with great patience in afflictions, in distress, in anguish, in battle, in prison, in rebellion, in hard labor, in vigil, in fasting." (2 Cor. 6: 4.5)

We stand on, bet everything - and win everything
You can interrupt the prayer process, but let the devil understand where you stand in the victory process. Let him clearly understand that you are coming back with strength and move on from where you were.

You can do this once you have broken through in the depths and found your position. But still, I would recommend you stand on until the whole victory is well in port. Remember you are the giant. Here you have to be completely conscious, be super clear on who you are in Christ - and stand and walk on that conviction.

The best thing, of course, is not to have any disruption in the process. But spend the time you need to get into the depth - and "tear" the victory out of Satan's claws and take it out into our soul / physical world. Have you now gone through the first round and calmed down your mind and feelings, and defeated everything that will prevent you from moving on.

Then you are ready for round 2
You have spent hours or maybe days on this process. This requires a great deal of commitment to make. When you first get started, you are glad you are committed to getting to the bottom. Then you will find that you will not be anywhere else but right here.

Now you're ready for the depth

The beast in the deep - you go ahead - Satan
backs
Now you meet Satan in the depths. You go forward all the time. As you go forward, the devil
backs. He backs every step you take. Do you
stop, he stops. If you go back, he'll follow. This
happens every time, these are my own experiences. NB! When you have victory in the flesh,
have everything in the light, and are protected by
the blood of Jesus Christ, you can be bold and
bold as a giant.
Then you command Satan and the demons who
are with him to leave the victim and never come
back.

Faith that does not falter
You do this only once and sign with "in the name
of Jesus". Now all the victory of Christ is behind
you. The victory that has been there for 2000

years has now been revealed to you. Remember: The command is given only once. If you do it again, you show the devil that you do not trust the Lord and His Word, and the devil attacks. Do not let go, victory is yours in Jesus name.

Follow-up:

NB! What you do as a follower: You still go against Satan, but now you praise the Lord for the victory that is now a fact! Now you accept nothing else, no matter what your circumstances tell you. Go out against Satan aggressively. You are the giant in the name of Jesus. Build a victory wall - which stands for all time.

The giant's strength

"All that is born of God overcomes the world, and this is the victory that overcomes the world, our faith." (1 John. 5,4)

Now you must stand firm in your faith. Now you must have the invisible to the eye, not the visible. The visible is temporal, the invisible is eternal and victorious. This is where your spiritual strength is to be displayed, and during your walk, more and more is developing. "Now that we have not the visible eye, but the invisible, for the visible is temporal, but the invisible is eternal." (2 Cor. 4:18)

We hold on to the invisible - and gain the victory in the visible
All of our trust, faith, conviction for God is in Jehovah's written promises.
They are applicable from the death of Christ on our behalf. His perfect victory over Satan and his demons for all eternity.

20

You must use your God-given authority with courage

It was said of Jesus: "As soon as all the people saw Him, they were horrified and rushed to salute Him. He asked them: What are you tired of? And one of the people answered, Master, I have brought to them my son, who is possessed by a mute spirit. And when he grabs it, it tugs at him, and he frets and cuts teeth and fades away. I asked your disciples to drive it out and they were not able to. Jesus answered them and said, you unbelieving kin, how long shall I endure you? Bring him here to Me! " (Mark. 9,15-19)

Read all the verses and you will see that Jesus with His simple, determined authority made the demon go. In the same way, when the assumption is met, it is with us that we have talked about here. You exercise God's power in Jesus' name on the ground of the Atonement, in humility and purity. Satan and the demons must go. It is an absolute event that will happen. I say it again: Go aggressively towards the devil. Die in your own performances. Go hard as steel against Satan, for victory is yours in Jesus name!

Let Satan rage with all his thoughts and feelings. You're stuck. Do not be thrown and driven by the weather of any doctrine - Satan's false thoughts and feelings.

"Stand firm." (Eph. 4:14)

Satan does not give up until he is in the sea of fire and brimstone, where he is tormented night and day forever.

Hold the grip - and go out with the win

Now you can leave the battle area. Stand firm in faith and victory. Then Satan and the demons will not come again. Let the security in you be absolute. Satan will make some projections, through thoughts, feelings, and other people. When he sees the tool (your absolute safety and attitude), he sticks.

Western Norway, 1975 - the demons are coming out

I remember on one occasion; a woman would be set free from demons. She expected a long episode of expulsion. I commanded the demons to leave her, in a few words - and in Jesus name. I turned and left the woman. I just had came a few meters away and stood with his back - then I heard the demons scream in the woman, and they all came out. The woman was free!

I have experienced this all over the world. As you do this, Satan knows that Jesus is there, so victory comes much quicker than in the beginning. There are great opportunities for overcoming life, for anyone who knows the call for a service like this.

A service like this will cost you everything

You must be willing to live a life of trials, failures, misunderstandings and suffering. This is not something you just "try". It's not just a simple snap of your finger and say, I'm more than a conqueror in Him, because the Bible says so. The Bible's words must be obeyed, obeyed, so that we are in the right position to live as the giant - the victor.

"All that is born of God overcomes the world, and this is the victory that has overcome the world, our faith." (1 John. 5.4)

The authority is ours in the name of Jesus
Jesus said, "If you stay in Me and My Words stay in you, pray for what you want and you will receive it." (John 15:17)

The authority is given to us when the conditions are met. When we do ours - the whole sky is standing in our backs with help. Praise the Lord for victory. I say it again: We do not have the visible to the eye, but the invisible.
The visible is temporal, the invisible is eternal. Stand firm, praise the Lord, victory is ours.

Barriers to stop victory
in the depths

The person who wants redemption must really want redemption

The person must have a deep desire for it, and after the deliverance the desire with all his heart to live fully for Christ, so that the rebirth can remain a fact. It is of great importance to be baptized in the Holy Spirit and fire quickly afterwards. And again, to learn to keep their freedom through the Bible. (I write this in detail in my book "Really Free"). If the person who wants deliverance does not want it, there will only be a trial of empty barrels rattling with no result.

Also, if it is not taken seriously after the deliverance, the spirit expelled will bring with it seven other spirits, worse than themselves.
(Matt. 12,43-45)

So, we see that this must be done seriously by the one who is a servant of the Lord and in earnest for the one who wants deliverance. Now I have mentioned a little about a direct confrontation with the one who wants deliverance. What we are discussing in this book is intercession in depth. The spiritual principles for the exercise of the spiritual work are always the same.

The indirect confrontation - prayer in the deep

We arrange for the aggrieved person, so that he or she has the opportunity to make a choice. Choices to receive Jesus as his Savior. Expulsion of demons is easier when in close contact with the person in question.

Calling in advance to clarify things for both parties is a very important tool. Great things can be accomplished at a long distance, even when praying in the depths, only by adhering to the Word of God. But nothing is like being present with the afflicted person.

Build a victory wall that always stands

After deliverance: Live a consciously surrendered life to Christ. Build a close love relation-

ship with Him. Stay close to His heart forever.
Let Christ remain the most important thing in
your whole life, let Him be your everything.
That's what He should be for all of us. He is the
LIFE. (John. 3,16 14,6)

"For our weapons of war are not carnal, but
mighty for God to overthrow fortifications, overthrowing the buildings of thought and every
height that rise up against the knowledge of God,
and captivating every thought under obedience
to Christ." (2 Cor. 10: 4-5)

Build up solidly with God's written Word
Carefully develop your love relationship with
Christ. Let His life always shines through you,
as a humble tool for Him. "And grasp, besides
all this shield of faith, by which you shall be able
to extinguish all the burning arrows of evil. And
take the helmet of salvation and the sword of the
Spirit, which is the Word of God. As you pray in
the Spirit at all times with all prayer and invocation. " (Eph. 6.16-18)

You are invincible only as long as you guard the wall

The wall keeper lives close to the heart of Christ and in covenant with the Word of God. Satan does not give up until he is in the eternal torments of perdition - but then he is there forever. He is forever defeated, and his time is carefully measured. Our time as the children of the Lord is eternal. There is no easy way - but that is the way.

22

Pray in the Spirit for Spirit
Pray in the flesh for spirit

We can be at prayer meetings; we can pray correctly - but do we get answers to prayer? Suddenly one day a light dawned on me about this. What happens if I pray in the flesh, in the sensual versus the spiritual, for prayer answers? I heard I said to myself: Nothing is happening! We live in the New Testament era (and well into it), we have passed the problems of the Middle Ages and come into greater light in the Word. We understand more and more of the Word, but does it help us if we just pray from the flesh against the spirit? Do we not use spiritual weapons against spiritual enemies?

Paul says, "Walk in the Spirit, and do not fulfill the lusts of the flesh!

For the flesh lusts against the Spirit, and the Spirit against the flesh. They oppose each other so you don't do what you want. " (Gal. 5, 17)

The confusion comes into the field
Here we see that confusion also comes into the field.
It is Satan, out of the spiritual, who comes with what we then accept in the flesh. The Lord requires in His Word that if we truly want to serve Him, He must be Lord in our lives and that we then obey His leadership.

Then these words from Paul are excellent: "If you confess Christ as Lord with your mouth, and believe in your heart that God raised Him from the dead, then you will be saved." (Rom. 10: 9)

Jesus as Lord is a first necessity! Not the flesh as Lord, but Christ, in His Spirit. Hear what Jesus said to the disciples:

"If you stay in Me and My Words stay in you, ask for what you want and you will get it."
(John. 15,7)

What is he saying? Yes, walk in My Spirit. We pray in the Spirit, we pray in the Holy Spirit of God, the victorious Spirit - and defeat the spirit of Satan. So be conscious in the Holy Spirit as you pray for answers. "For our weapons of war are not carnal, but mighty for God to overthrow fortifications, overthrowing the buildings of thought and every height that rise up against the knowledge of God, and captivating every thought under obedience to Christ." (2 Cor 10,5)

Fighting in the spirit is fighting with thoughts - thoughts are spiritual

"When Jesus saw your thoughts, He said, Why are you thinking so badly in your hearts?" (Matt. 9,4)

Jesus looked into the spirit and saw their thoughts: "But when Jesus knew their thoughts ..." (Matt. 12:25) "

But there was a thought in them about who was the biggest among them. But when Jesus saw the thought of their hearts..." (Luke. 9:46-47)

It's not hard to understand, the revelation is so up in the day. To a large extent, it is in this way, in mind, that Satan attacks - and we must "take him" with God's Word. We just have to make sure we are in the Spirit, so that the Spirit of God in us (and the Word) goes against Satan's spirit - and wins victory.

Most Christians do not connect thought to the spiritual at all
They think that thoughts are thoughts. Yes, that's right, but they're spiritual. All our thoughts, however, are spiritual. Thoughts and emotions are an important component of our spiritual life. They cannot be separated. Every thought gives a feeling and every feeling gives a thought.

Disruptions in the mindset when praying are demonic. Disruptions in the thinking life are spiritual, so treat it accordingly.

2 3

Bring out your victories
in the spiritual world

Deep prayer in GT (before the Atonement) under other conditions, led by God Jehovah's Spirit

We read from 1 King:

"Then Elijah said to Ahab," Go up now and have a drink! Because I hear the rain buzzing. Then Ahab went up to eat and drink. But Elijah rose to the top of Carmel and bowed to the ground with his face between his knees. Then he said to his boy: Get up and look out to the sea! And he went up and looked, but said, There is nothing to see. Seven times he said: Go there again! On the seventh day he said, Behold, a little cloud, as great as a man's hand, rises from the sea. And he said, Go up and say unto Ahab, Stretch and go down, lest the rain be upon you. And in a turning, the sky blackened with clouds and with a storm, and a heavy rain came; And Ahab went and went to Jezreel. But the hand of the Lord came upon Elijah, and he encircled his loins, and ran before Ahab, even unto Jezreel. " (1 King 18,41-46)

Here we see a fine example from GT about going deep into prayer, under other conditions than we have today. That did not prevent God from having His ways of exercising His will, as we see here through the prophets.

Elijah entered the spirit, purposefully, in faith and expectation - until victory came
And it came! Of course, the Lord had taught Elijah the prophet in training and testing for years, before the great tasks and spiritual understanding came.
Here we see he had divine energy over his physical body in such a way that he ran in front of the horses of Ahab all the way to Jezreel!
Imagine what you can accomplish in the deep prayer that you are now heading into. This will be like an adventure for you, and you will no longer desire anything but to be in prayer in the Spirit.

Deep prayer in the garden of Gethsemane, we will look at this again

Let's go to Jesus in prayer in the Garden of Gethsemane: "And Jesus wiped himself from them as far as a stone's throw, fell to his knees, prayed, and said: Father if you will, let this lime pass me by! Horever, My will not happen, but yours! And He came in fear of death and prayed even more fiercely, and His sweat became like drops of blood, falling to the ground. "
(Luke, 22, 41-44)

Here we see Jesus in deep prayer, the last prayer before the crucifixion. He purposefully entered the world of the Spirit, and He knew so well how to do it. He had to do it to meet God and talk to Him. This became so concentrated and powerful that His sweat became like drops of blood. Here Jesus made the final big decision, which in turn led Him to the cross of Calvary where He completed the work He had come to do - the wonderful miracle of redemption for you and me. It is in the depths of the Spirit and prayer that we get the answers and receive guidance from God.

And He came in fear of death and prayed even more fiercely, and His sweat became like drops of blood, falling to the ground. "
(Luke. 22, 41-44)

Here we see Jesus in deep prayer, the last prayer before the crucifixion. He purposefully entered the world of the Spirit, and He knew so well how to do it. He had to do it to meet God and talk to Him. This became so concentrated and powerful that His sweat became like drops of blood. Here Jesus made the final big decision, which in turn led Him to Calvary's cross where He completed the work He had come to do - the wonderful miracle of redemption for you and me. It is in the depths of the Spirit and prayer that we get the answers and receive guidance from God.

Deep prayer on the cross
"Then, when Jesus knew that now everything was complete, for the Scriptures to be fulfilled, He says: I thirst. There was a tub full of vinegar, then they put a sponge full of the vinegar on an isop stalk and held it up to His mouth. When Jesus had received the vinegar, He said, "It is fin-

ished!" And He bowed His head and gave up the spirit. " (John.19, 28-30)

Here in Jesus' last minute, just before He gives up His spirit, we see that He is in the physical and the spiritual. Here, the line of communication in the spirit is open to God, while He is also conscious in the physical.

Jesus knew it was complete
Here we see Jesus in the physically conscious, where He oversees the situation and sees that everything goes according to Scripture so that it is fulfilled. Jesus now entered into the Spirit, took upon Himself all the sin of the world, and was made atonement for Your and My sins. Then out in the physical consciousness, He says, "It is finished!"
And He gives up the spirit. He gives His life for humanity.
The eternal last great victory is won!

There are 3 ways to get prayer answers in the physical over world:

I explain victory over demons. It is done the same way with all kinds of prayers for an answer.

1

In the prayer closet we bind the demon in the actual person

We **bind** the demons in the spirit, and **command the demon to leave the person when we give the command.** The command we give when we are with the person in the natural world. Then the answer will come.

2

In the physical world of flesh, we lose or release the person from the demon

We have bound the current demon in the spirit. We do this in the spirit in the prayer closet. Furthermore, in the physical world we release the person in whom we have bound the demon. We do not bind the demon here, it has already been done in the spirit world, when we were in the prayer closet. Now we release or lose the person in the physical world from the demon.

3 We know what we are doing

We are conscious of our state of mind in the spirit, while we are in the physical, the demon is already bound, so we lose the person from the demon there in the natural/physical world.

All these prayers always end with the signature "in the name of Jesus".

Disease spirits that go straight to the body

There is another department of sickness spirit that goes straight on with attack to the body. Some from the outside and into the body, while others can again come through thoughts from demons and into our thought life (into our personality/soul). Here the person must accept the thought from Satan. If the person accepts then the actual sickness moves into the body.

We pray and believe with the obedience of faith with the Word of God in the Spirit, and defeat the demons in the spirit - and the result comes in the physical.

24

Do you want to hear the voice of God?

If you want to hear the voice of God, you must enter the world of the Spirit. You must understand that thoughts are spiritual. All "disturbing" thoughts that come to you, no matter how ordinary and personal, are from Satan - who does not want you to calm down thoughts and feelings and discern/understand where the thoughts come from. It may take a long time for the Lord, offensively, before it begins to stabilize understanding of this for you. You must be able to distinguish between the Word of God in your world of thought and your own words (your inner voice). If you manage to put everything to a standstill in your emotions and thoughts, keep calm for a second, you will hear the voice of God. Now that you understand how to distinguish the Word of God from your words in your

mind (in your mind), you are on the right path. Remember, for the Lord is a day like a thousand years. He can tell you what He wants in one second. What is one second to you is about 21/2 days for the Lord. (From the calculus where a thousand years is one day).
When you find the second, then comes the thought/voice from God.
There are no prayer shelves, Jericho marches, and war tongues. This is the reality. I am writing this to show you that time, place and space are infinite in God Jehovah.

The reality of silence with God
The reality is in the silence with God, where you are helpless and defenseless. You yearn and depend on hearing from God so that your life can live to its full potential, in His will. Here in this one second, the Lord can give you all the information you need.

Find calm before moving on - pray in tongues
"He who speaks in tongues builds himself up."
(1 Cor. 14: 4)

Do you want to hear the voice of God?

If you want to hear the voice of God, you must enter the world of the Spirit. You must understand that thoughts are spiritual. All "disturbing" thoughts that come to you, no matter how ordinary and personal, are from Satan - who does not want you to calm down thoughts and feelings and discern/understand where the thoughts come from. It may take a long time for the Lord, offensively, before it begins to stabilize understanding of this for you. You must be able to distinguish between the Word of God in your world of thought and your own words (your inner voice). If you manage to put everything to a standstill in your emotions and thoughts, keep calm for a second, you will hear the voice of God. Now that you understand how to distinguish the Word of God from your words in your mind (in your mind), you are on the right path.

Remember for the Lord is a day like a thousand years

He can tell you what He wants in one second. What is one second to you is about 21/2 days for the Lord. (From the calculation I found that a thousand years is one day). When you find the second, then comes the thought/voice.

There are no prayer shaking, Jericho marches, and war tongues. This is the reality. I am writing this to show you that time, place and space are infinite in God Jehovah.

The reality of silence with God
The reality is in the silence with God, where you are helpless and defenseless. You yearn and depend on hearing from God so that your life can live to its full potential, in His will. Here in this one second, the Lord can give you all the information you need.

Find the peace in yourself before moving on - pray in tongues

"He who speaks in tongues builds himself up." (1 Cor. 14: 4)

As you enter the prayer in this way, you can calm down before proceeding. If something disturbing has appeared or you need some rest in the advance, you can pray in tongues inside you. Then you go back on, work consciously to get thoughts and feelings to settle down completely. Pray in tongues and work to keep all thoughts quiet. Even thinking that it will be quiet is also a thought - and it must and must be calmed down.

Prayer closet - prayer in the Holy Spirit

Let's take a look at how to get into the "chamber of prayer - prayer".

Salary chamber - prayer means Peace in small space, in the human interior. Prayer closet have a lot of different meanings from the original tongue.

"And Jesus said unto them, come ye now with me aside, into a desert place, and rest a little." (Mark. 6,31)

"Jesus says, but when you pray, go into your chamber; And when you close your door, pray to your Father who is in hiding. And your Father who sees in secret will pay you openly. " (Matt. 6.6)

Exercise: Close the gates of the senses - put the meat to rest

"Walk in the Spirit, and do not fulfill the requests of the flesh. For the flesh lusts against the Spirit and the Spirit against the flesh. They op-

pose each other, so you don't do what you want. But if you are driven by the Spirit, you are not under the law. But the fruits of the Spirit are love, joy, peace, longsuffering, gentleness, goodness, faithfulness, meekness, and abstinence. Against such, the law is not. "
(Gal 5, 16.18.23)

"The spirit of man is a lamp of the Lord; it searches everything within the human being."
(Proverbs 20, 27)

"And six days after that, Jesus took with him Peter, and James the brother of John, and led them away on a high mountain. And He was explained to their eyes, and His face shone like the sun, and His clothes became white as the light.
" (Matt 16,1.2)

We read further in Luke: "Jesus said to His disciples: I surrender the kingdom to you, as My Father delivered it to Me, so that you may eat and drink at My table in My kingdom."
(Luke. 22, 29-30)

"He raised us with Him, and set us with Him in heaven, in Christ Jesus." (Eph. 2.6)

The psalmist says, "The Lord of hosts is with us; The God of Jacob is our permanent city.
" (Psalm 46: 8)

"Against the power of the mighty enemy, I will beseech Thee, for God is my Stronghold." (Psalm 59, 10)

At the Lord's table - the table in the secret chamber, in the Spirit

"Jesus said to His disciples," I surrender the kingdom to you, as My Father delivered it to Me, so that you may eat and drink at My table in My kingdom. " (Luke. 22, 29.30)

"He raised us with Him, and set us with Him in heaven, in Christ." (Eph. 2.6)

"And by faith in Him, we have access with confidence ..." We now share company with Moses, Aaron, Nadab, Abihu and the 70 of Israel's elders who ate at the Lord's table on Mount Sinai. (Eph. 3,12)

"And they saw the God of Israel. Under His feet, it was like a floor of transparent sapphire stone, clear as the sky itself. He does not raise His hand

to the foremost of the children of Israel, but they beheld God - and ate and drank. "
(Exodus 24: 10.11)

"When David became king, he made a seat at his table for Jonathan's son, Mephibosheth: Don't be afraid, I will do good to you for your father Jonathan's sake ... you will always eat at my table." (2 Sam. 9,2)

How to get to the Lord's table in the secret chamber, in the spirit?

Now we are talking about stepping into an area of the spiritual world where God has the meeting place between Him and us. The meeting place in the Holy Spirit, in the spirit world. If we are to enter here, we must get out of the senses and the dominant world of the flesh, and into the spiritual world. God Jehovah, the world.

Your paycheck is inside you

There is a groundbreaking dimension that is inside you, while at the heavenly place outside the universes. We have the meeting place inside us, which at the same time is millions of light-years away from the place we once travel to. Relax completely - believe this. That's the way it is. You are entering a whole new life and a whole new dimension.

How to get into the prayer closet?

To enter "your chamber", the prayer closet in your spirit. You must consciously cut off the ability of the deeds of the flesh to influence you. And you may have to repent with all your heart, from the deeds of the flesh that have been a problem for you. Then consciously close the entrance doors of the senses to you, from the world of the senses around you. Now concentrate on God Jehovah

listen and see in the Spirit. listen and see in the Spirit.

2 6

The war is on

State your feelings and thoughts. Now the emotion and the influence of the thoughts on you must bc complctcly rcstcd so that you will be able to hear the speech of God (the Holy Spirit). Now special thoughts are hammering into your mind, which requires deep concentration to disappear. You have to let go of the thought that they will disappear, because it is also a thought. This will be a training session that will take a long time. In this long process, you will begin to experience new things emerging in your prayer life. Experiences to come before reaching full victory in this.

A whole new world will open up to you. Your experience and your way of being in prayer will in many things be different from the experiences of others. This is very personal and therefore very individual.

157

The psalmist says, "God spoke, and it happened
- He commanded, and it stood there."
(Psalm 33: 9)

"But this one, do not blind you, beloved, that one
day is in the eyes of the Lord as a thousand years
and a thousand years as a day." (2 Pet. 3,8)

If we can manage for one second to be free from
thoughts (which are spiritual), then the Lord is
there with His speech and can tell you a thousand years of history in one second. Which dimensions, they are straight out divine.

The battle of the mind is with thoughts - and
thoughts are spiritual
The Bible says, "Behold, besides all this, the
shield of faith, which will extinguish all the
burning arrows of the wicked one." (Eph 6.16)

So we see that the enemy's weapons are arrows
of thought. He does not want you to calm it
down so that you can hear the voice of God. But
you can - with training.

A spiritual election campaign

To get through the last resistance at the moment, you must believe that it is the Lord who speaks to you in your thoughts. Here come Satan's thought arrows again. Here you have to put things away until you find peace and focus on what you want to believe. Do you think you are inside?

Extensive additions

From the physical world and into the spiritual world, in the Holy Spirit

Acquiring an intellectual understanding of theological topics is only a small step in the right direction. At least one must have a clear understanding of God's Word that can point one in the right direction so that one can begin the walk. Who has the opportunity?

A converted, reborn, baptized in the Holy Spirit man, who again lives in the written Word of God. Have all the opportunities to have a close relationship with the Father, the Son and the Holy Spirit in the spiritual reality outside of our physical world. This is something that should be natural for any born-again Christian.

The two things that are connected

There are two things that are completely insepa-
rable, we find them in the mission command. I
mention here Mark. 16, 15.

"Go out into the world and preach the gospel to
all creation." (Mark. 16, 15)

World

The word "world" from Greek and Hebrew has
several completely different meanings. I mention
the meaning of Cosmos, which is all universes.
The universe of which our galaxy is a small part
is not one of the largest universes.

There are several universes besides the one we
are part of. Planet Earth is the fifth smallest
planet in the galaxy named Milky Way.
Av andre betydninger av ordet verden har
vi **evighetenes evighet**, vi har **evighetens
evighets tid og rom**.

Utenfor alt dette, antar jeg at vi har himlenes
rike og Guds trone. Nå blir forståelsen av ordet"
verden" større.

Creature

Man is the creature. We are created in the image of God. It is not our physique, but it is our spirit. "God is spirit." (John 4:24) It is the invisible to the physical eye, part of us. Our body is shaped, formed and built of soil (Adama from Hebrew). (Genesis 2, 7)

In Mark. 16, 15 there are two tasks in the word "world", one is the gospel of Jesus Christ to all creation and the other to all the cosmos with all its time and space.

The two work areas

Warfare from Earth and on Earth. Here is our mission to preach the gospel so that all creatures have the opportunity to hear it. In this proclamation of the gospel, we perform the spiritual warfare on earth, which is then to carry out the tasks Mark. 16, 17 - 18 leads us to.

"And these signs must follow those who believe: In my name, in the name of Jesus, they will drive out evil spirits, they will speak with tongues.

They should take snakes in their hands, and if they drink something poisonous, it will not harm them. In sick they will lay their hands and they will be healed. " (Mark 16, 17-18)

Victories on earth, giving victories in the spirit world in the Cosmos

These are the tools for waging spiritual warfare on earth. This will give effect to the earth through physical victories, such as healings, humans being set free from demons. This, in turn, will give effect to victories in the spirit world outside the cosmos.

The war in Kosmos

Now we come to what the Bible calls prayer. The word prayer has many different meanings also from the basic Hebrew and Greek languages.

We have the prayers that we know most, which are different types of intercession. As we come to the chamber of prayer - prayer, we begin to approach what I now want to mention.

27

Different type of "prayer"
in the prayer room

We have "Paga" which means to attack, confront.

"Daras" which means search and visit.

"Tehinna" means humble.

In humbleness before God, His Word and the spiritual world, we seek until we have located the enemy. When the enemy is located, we attack.

We attack and win the victory that has already been won. We let the enemy understand that we know what we have of spiritual resources and authority.

Attacks in humility

Now I come into a kind of prayer of confrontation and attack in humility in the spirit world. This is certainly not practiced with loud cries.

On the other hand, we know who we are, know what we are doing and know what we have come to in the areas of Kosmos. Here we come in only because the Lord has led us here. Our position here is listening as we perform the tasks. The Lord will guide each one personally. Here it is talk of winning victories in the spirit that has an impact on the physical on earth.

How to be led here - how to get started

I would like to mention some simple guidelines to get you started. Insight into truth must be experienced personally. In the Western world, which is the Christian world, we have been bound and locked in so many religious forms that have been imposed upon us over generations. Things that have become part of us, without us noticing. This, in turn, has made us unbelievers of spiritual realities.

We have let circumstances govern us, instead of the word of God

The beliefs of the West (the Christian part of the world) have been based on the circumstances, as the senses have shown us. Not on the Word of God, which in turn originates from the spiritual world in the Cosmos and beyond into the Kingdom of God etc.

The Word of God is our only guideline and Jesus Christ who is the Son of God is ours and the Savior of the world.

The prayer closet and past the prayer closet

We must go into our secret chamber with God alone. We must seek him in silence until we find him. We must have a real repentance and put the flesh's activities behind us. Only this is a daunting job, but this must be done first if it takes years. It must be silence from your own flesh, which is your contact to the earth.

When in place, we embark on the search for God in the spirit world

Now we go in search of God in prayer. Here there must be complete silence. Not only silence with words, but silence in the mind, in this position we must work to gradually bring the mind to rest. We must allow God's thought to let go.

Spiritual warfare

Here, Satan's thought arrows will also try to get to. This is spiritual warfare. Satan will do everything he can to stop you from getting through here. All the processes you are about to embark on will be your learning. Learning with the Lord is always personal and hard. Here in the process, you will learn to cope and socialize with the thought life. You will learn everything necessary to do and how to do the details according to your beliefs.

Faith a master key

Faith is a top priority for moving forward in the spirit world. It is the door opener going forward in this adventure. You will learn the importance of faith in precision in time and place. You have to believe at the moment. If you do not hit, you must start the work again. Whoever gives up has lost, the one who does not give up already has the victory.

Your first big win will be in the mindset

The Mind life is the gateway to the world of the spirit and the gateway to the physical world. Now you will learn to discern between the Spirit of God, the Holy Spirit and the Word of God to you, the spirit and words of Satan to you and your own thoughts and feelings.

The learning here comes as you gradually learn how to discern and obey right. This can go on for a long time. You will be locked away thought after thought and gradually learn to arrest thoughts and recognize thoughts.

Now I'm not talking about the sinful thoughts of the flesh. It is now a laid-back stage. It was already behind you when you first began your search this way. Every battle in the world of the spirit takes place in the realm of thought.

When it finally gets quiet in the mind

You can move out in faith. Everything takes place in faith. Here is no use in trying, unbelief or say: I think it works now. The trait of faith is so, when you believe it, you do it.

Before you even think of faith. Faith is established and works on automation. There is learning at every little point. Wrong and right. It takes months and years to get solid into this. When you come in, it becomes a world you walk in every day, out and in. You just have to seek to get into the position.

This is what Jesus did in the mountains alone at night

"And when Jesus had let the people go, he went up into the mountain to pray; and when evening came, he was there alone.

Jesus had to go through all things as a natural human being. He had to seek contact with the Father as a natural human being must. He was a pioneer for us in absolutely every detail.

But the boat was all in the middle of the sea and worked hard against the waves, for the wind was against. But in the fourth watch of the night he came to them, wandering on the sea. And when the disciples saw him water upon the sea, they were astonished, saying, it is a ghost, and they cried out with fear.

Here we see Jesus from the miraculous to the silent, and to the miraculous again. Jesus had trained his entrance and quick presence to God the Father, which you can also do, by leading the way to establish it. God wants a constant close relationship with you.

But Jesus immediately spoke to them, saying, Be bold; it's me, fear not!

Then Peter answered him and said, Lord! if it is you, invite me to come to you on the water!

Jesus said, come! And Peter got out of the boat and went across the water to come to Jesus.
" (Matt. 14, 23-29)

You can live consciously on earth and in the spiritual world at the same time filled with the power of the Holy Spirit.

2 8

Are you ready?

You must first make sure that you live in full victory, in your own life. If you do, you know it. The victory you carry in you is the victory you can bring out of you to help others. You have to know, which is a step further than believing. You must live in the realm of conviction with your faith, in Christ Jesus and His work of Atonement on Calvary.

There must not be a shadow of doubt in you There must not be a shadow of doubt in your spiritual existence regarding these things. You must know without a doubt that the victory Christ Jesus won was for you and all other people who were born and live or have lived on planet earth (Tellus).

When Jesus knew that everything was complete

"Then when Jesus knew that now everything was complete, for the writing to be fulfilled, he says: I thirst.

There was a tub full of vinegar, they then put a sponge full of vinegar on an isop stalk and held it up to his mouth.

And when Jesus had received the vinegar, he said, it is finished. And he bowed his head and gave up the spirit. " (John. 19, 28-30)

You are the giant in the spirit with a foundation unshakable at the Atonement, which goes into the spirit, wars and wins the war. You have to know what you do; you have the full certainty of what you do.

"For all that is begotten of God overcomes the world, and this is the victory that overcomes the world; our faith. " (I John. 5, 4)

You never have more victory outward than you have inward. The victory you live daily in your own life is the victory you can exert to other people. Nothing more than that. If you live here, then - Are you ready?

Preparation

You need to check yourself out if everything in your life is in the light. Go before the Lord and check your conscience. See that everything is fine. If you have any satanic snares on you, you are not ready for a task like this. Then the demons will see the opportunity to jump on you too.

If you have all the things in the light, ask Jesus' blood for protection. Let the blood shield of Christ cover you.

They triumphed over him, Satan, by the blood of the lamb and the word they testified.

The Bible says, "And they have triumphed over him, Satan by the blood of the lamb, and the word they testified, and they had not loved, even unto death." (Rev. 12.11)

Christ, with His own blood, won an eternal redemption and Satan was forever a defeated enemy. The precious pure blood of Jesus Christ is testified on the mercy seat in heaven as the eternal covenant blood, with an eternally defeated Satan in the lake of fire - think forever.

Heb. says, "And not with the blood of goats and calves, but with his own blood, once into the sanctuary, and found eternal redemption."
(Heb. 9, 2)

Without blood being shed, no remission occurs "And almost everything is cleansed with blood according to the law, and without blood being shed, forgiveness does not happen." (Heb. 9, 22)

Are you here now,
Then Satan knows you and you know him, the preparation is done. You are the giant who goes into the depths of humility, but with authority in the name of Jesus.

John says, "All that is born of God overcomes the world, and this is the victory that overcome the world, our faith." (1 John. 5, 4)

Go forward

As you now move forward towards Satan, you never stop. If you stop, he starts to push, you can then be tilted back to back in the fight. Go ahead all the time. When you go against, go against and go to victory. Look through, to win all the time. Through Satan and the demons, you do not stop in front of them, you constantly move forward and through to victory.

Our victory was won 2,000 years ago, but Satan has wrongfully taken our territories because we have not claimed our rights in Christ. Now it's finally over, we're not giving Satan room.

Ephesians says: "Do not allow Satan"
(Eph. 4: 27).

Take Your Right In the Spirit (1 Tim. 3, 16)
As Jesus won perfectly right in the spirit world on Calvary's cross, in faith you take out the vic-

tory and judgment in Jesus that he won for you on Calvary.

What you have to do now is demand your right, simple and easy. Satan has had this privilege of ours without being disturbed for so long, and has seen so many weak Christians that he has not cared about.

When a giant like you comes, he is not used to such things, he has only seen weak Christians. He thinks you are easily matched, but gets shocked when he sees you. You just go ahead and don't plan to stop. Satan knows he has "trouble". You go ahead. Remember! People around you are Satan's first choice of tools to break you. Be careful who you have around you. Only have the "believers fighting around you" Those who can lift you, not push down.

On the road into the depths

Now when you enter your paycheck alone or together with others. For the first time, I recommend you go into the prayer closet alone. You must go several times alone in the pay room. Then you quickly find out whether you should always be in the payroll alone or with someone.

I think it will be alone, but support may be good in the beginning.

You must obtain and understand your position and place in the spirit. This may take time. Remember you are the giant of Christ Jesus. Bend your knees and close your eyes. Or another position that is comfortable for you.

Enter the prayer closet alone

When you walk into your secret chamber alone, this is your personal sanctuary, your personal arena, where you have sat down with God. God is spirit and you must have contact with him in the spiritual world. This is wherein the spiritual world also Satan moves, so this is where we meet him and his demons. This is where you learn Satan's way of working. You can reveal him and defeat him.

Make sure your paycheck is free of distracting sound, visual impressions, yes, all things that may appeal to your senses. Close the shutters to the windows of the senses and open the shutters inward in the spirit.

Now there is no outside impression that we should concentrate on. Now that is the spiritual world alone, we seek the greatest possible contact with it to fulfill our mission.

It is also here in the spirit that we develop our most intimate relationship with God. Here in the spirit, there are several arenas you want to get to know.

Concentrate on the work of calming down your soul

Now you have to want your life in full. The first thing you do is lift all the deeds of the flesh out in the distance, you see it out there, you have control over it.

You put your soul/personality under the control of your will. If you control this, you live in victory over the flesh.

No room for the meat

If it turns out that you have problems in areas of your flesh, then it must be fixed in its entirety and gained victory over and survived in victory over. Before you try what, we are doing now. You will not enter into any of this without victory in your own life. On the other hand, you will be winking at the demons. There is even more trouble than you have had so far.

But if the victory in your life is clear, then you move on.

Under the authority of the Lord

Now you consciously leave your will under the authority of the Lord. Now you are starting to get disciplined and calmed down your personality/soul. This is 100% necessary.

Satan will do everything he can to upset you. He doesn't want you to win the victory here, so you can move on into the spirit. Remember, we live in a spiritual world first and foremost

The spiritual battle is on

The devil tries to knock you out at startup. Can you see what I'm talking about? I know you do. All spiritual attacks come through our emotions and thoughts, with desires and other disturbing thoughts. This is the only way the devil can contact you, yes disturb you. Satan will attack you in your life, through emotions and thoughts. Everything in your life is stored on your hard drive, in your soul / personality. Here Satan is fishing. Therefore, all sensory impressions to you must possibly be stopped by you, you must with your will life calm down everything you can of your feelings and thoughts.

Thoughts and feelings always go against each other. What you feel, you think. What you think you feel.

The devil does not want you to go into the depths of the Spirit

This must be clear to you. Here you will win your victories - in depth

Once the victory is won here in the personality / soul arena, you are ready to move on.

The battle of the soul / personality can last for hours after hours. Are you ready for this or do you want to give up before you get started?

This may take days before you are ready for the dip. Not many are willing to do this. Fasting can be a help here. Feel free to go through the entire prayer process

In Gal, Paul says, "But I say, walk in the Spirit, and do not make the lusts of the flesh.

For the flesh lusts against the Spirit and the Spirit against the flesh. They oppose each other so you don't do what you want. " (Gal. 5, 16-17)

There are always some things, which don't even have to be that big. If there is something small or big in the meat, then there is an obstacle, now everything is focused on the victory.

Why fast?
Well, for one purpose, you get a greater concentration on the spiritual things,
than the concentration on the physical things.
You become much clearer in the soul
and the spiritual.
This is the sole purpose of fasting.

2 Cor. I think fits well in this context.

"But show us in all things as the servants of God, with great patience in afflictions, in distress, in anguish, in battle, in prison, in rebellion, in hard labor, in vigil, in fasting." (2 Cor. 6: 4-5)

We give all, and win all.

You can interrupt the prayer process
but let Satan understand where you stand in the process of victory, let him clearly understand

that you are coming back with strength and moving on from where you were.
You can do this once you have broken through in the depths and found your position. But still, I would recommend you to stand on until the whole victory is well in port.

Remember you are the giant
Here you have to be completely conscious, yes be super clear on who you are and what you are in Christ, stand, walk and live this conviction fully.
The best thing, of course, is not to have any interruption in the process, but spend the time you need to get into the depths to "tear" the victory out of Satan's claws and take it out into our soul / physical world.

Did you get through round 1?
Have you now gone through the first round and calmed down your mind and emotional life and defeated everything that will prevent you from moving on.

Then you are ready for round 2.

Have you now gone through the first round and calmed down your mind and emotional life and defeated everything that will prevent you from moving on.

You have spent hours or maybe days on this process. This requires a great deal of commitment to make. When you first get started, you are glad you are committed to getting through to the depth. Then you will find that you will not be anywhere else but right here.

Now you are "ready for the deep".
(Here's more to say, which I will include in collections and groups).

3 0

The beast in the deep - you go ahead - Satan backs

Now you meet Satan in the depths. You go forward all the time. As you go forward, the devil backs all the time, he backs for every step you take. Do you stop, he stops. If you go back, he'll follow. This happens every time, these are my own experiences since day one.

NB
When you have victory in the flesh, all in the light, and are protected by the blood of Jesus Christ, you can be bold and bold as a giant. You command Satan and the demons who are with him to leave the victim never to return.
You do this only once and sign with "in the name of Jesus". Now all the victory of Christ is behind you, the victory that has already been there for 2000 years has now come to revelation in this

case. Remember the command is given only once, if you do it again, you show the devil that you do not trust the Lord and his words and the devil attacks. Do not let go, victory is yours in Jesus name.

What you do as a sequel

NB What you do as a sequel. You still go against Satan, but now praise the Lord for the victory that is now a fact. Now you accept nothing else, no matter what your circumstances tell you.

Go aggressively towards the devil. You are the giant in the name of Jesus.
Build a wall of victory - which stands forever

Giant Strength (Your Strength)

All that is born of God overcomes the world, and this is the victory that has triumphed over the world, our faith.

We read, "All that is born of God overcomes the world, and this is the victory that overcomes the world, our faith" (1 John. 5, 4).

Now you must stand firm in your faith. Now you must have the invisible to the eye, not the visible, the visible is temporal, the invisible is eternal and victorious.

This is where your spiritual strength should be displayed and during your walk more and more developed knowledge.

2 Cor say, "So that we have not the visible, but the invisible, for the visible is temporal, but the invisible is eternal." (2 Cor. 4: 18)

We hold on to the invisible and gain victory in the visible.

We give all our confidence, faith, conviction to the written God of Jehovah (The Self-Existing Who Reveals) promises that apply from the death of Christ's Atonement to us and as the perfect victory over Satan and his demons for all eternity.

You must use your God-given authority in the command of Satan and the demons

Mark says: It was said of Jesus: "As soon as all the people saw him, they were astonished and ran to greet him. He asked them: What are you tired of? And one of the people answered, Master, I have brought to them my son, who is possessed by a mute spirit. And when it grabs it, it tugs at it, and it tears and cuts its teeth and fades away. I asked your disciples to drive it out and they were unable to.

Jesus answered them and said, "You unbelieving generation, how long shall I endure you before he comes to me" (Mark. 9, 15-19)

Read all the verses, then you see Jesus with a simple definite authority, got the demon to go.

In the same way it will be with us in depth, when the premise is met, which we talked about here. You exercise God's power in Jesus' name on the ground of the Atonement in humility and purity. Satan and the demons must go. It is an absolute event that will happen.

I say it again, go aggressively towards the devil

Those in your own imaginations, go hard as steal against Satan, victory is yours in Jesus name. Let Satan rage with all his thoughts and feelings. You're stuck. Don't be thrown and driven by the weather of any doctrine - yes, Satan's lie thoughts and feelings,

Ephesians the letter says, "Stand firm."
(Eph. 4:14)

Satan does not give up until he is in the sea of fire and brimstone where he is tormented night and day forever - but then he is there

Keep the grip going out with the victory

Now you can leave the battle area. Stand firm in faith and victory. Then Satan and the demons will not come again. Let the security in you be absolute. Satan will make some projections, through thoughts, feelings and other people. When he sees the utmost security and attitude of the implement, (you), he sticks.

Satan and the demons must obey

I remember on one occasion a woman would be delivered. She expected a long episode of expulsion. I commanded the demon to leave her in a few words Jesus' name, and I left the woman. I had only come a few meters away with my back. Then I heard the demons scream in the woman that they all came out. The woman was free.

I have experienced this all over the world since I was a young boy

As you do this, Satan knows that Jesus is with you, so victory comes much quicker than in the beginning.

There are great opportunities for a victorious life, for anyone who knows the call for a service like this. A service like this will cost you everything, it will cost you the life the same way every service of the Spirit of God does. You must be willing to live with, trials, despises, misunderstandings and suffering. This is not something you "try"

It's not just a simple snap of your finger and say: I'm more than a conqueror in Him, because the Bible says so. The Bible's words must be followed, yes obeyed so that we are in the position to live as the Giant - the victor.

"All that is born of God overcomes the world, and this is the victory that has overcome the world, our faith." (1 John. 5,4)

Yes, if you pay the price for it, the price is even the death of life.

Authority is ours in Jesus' name
Joh. Jesus said: If you stay in me and my words stay in you, pray for what you want and you will receive it. (John. 15:17)

The authority is given to us when the conditions are met.

When we do ours - the whole sky is standing in our backs with help. Praise the Lord for victory.

I say it again, we do not have the visible to the eye, but the invisible. The visible is temporal, the invisible is eternal. Stand firm, praise the Lord, victory is ours.

3 2

Barriers to victory in the depths

The person who wants redemption - must really want redemption. He must have a deep desire for it. Furthermore, after the deliverance, he or she must desire with all his heart to live completely for Christ, so that the rebirth can remain a fact. It is of great importance to be baptized in the Holy Spirit and fire soon afterward. And again, learning to keep their freedom through the Bible. I write this in a supplementary way in my book "Really Free".

If the person who wants deliverance does not want it, there will only be a trial of empty barrels rattling with no result. Also, if it is not taken seriously after the deliverance, the spirit expelled will carry with it seven other spirits, worse than oneself (Matt. 12: 43-45). Read this carefully.

So that we see and understand that this must be done seriously. It must be done with the seriousness of the one who serves in the Lord, and in earnest for the one who wants deliverance. Now I have mentioned a little about a direct confrontation with the one who wants deliverance. What we are discussing in this book is intercession in the depths, the spiritual principles for the exercise of the spiritual work always the same. (Here I use little to because I talk about spirituality in general. I talk about God the Spirit of God; it is with great O. Jehovah is the father of Jesus Christ).

In the indirect confrontation - Prayer in the deep

If we arrange for the plaintiff so that he or she has the opportunity to make a choice. Choices to receive Jesus as their Savior. Expulsion of demons is easier when in close contact with the person in question.

Advance talks to clarify for both parties are a very important tool. Great things can be accomplished at long distances even when praying in the depths, only if you keep to the word of God, the Bible.

But nothing is like being present with the person in question

Build the wall of victory that always stands

After deliverance, live a consciously surrendered life to Christ. Build a close love relationship with him. Stay forever alive close to his heart. Let Christ remain the most important thing in your whole life, let him be your everything. That's what he should be for all of us. He is life (John 3:16, John 14,6).

2 Corinthians says: "For our weapons of war are not carnal, but mighty for God to overthrow fortifications,
As we overthrow thought buildings and every height that rise against the knowledge of God, capturing every thought under obedience to Christ" (2 Cor. 10, 4 - 5)

Build up solidly with God's written word, live to develop your love relationship with Christ carefully. Let His life always shine through you, as a humble tool for Him.

Ephesians the letter says: And grasp besides all this shield of faith, that ye may devour all the burning arrows of the wicked.

And take the helmet of salvation and the sword
of the Spirit, which is the word of God.
As you pray in the Spirit at all times with all
prayer and invocation " (Eph. 6: 16-18)

**You are invincible only as long as you guard
the wall.**
The wall keeper lives close to the heart of Christ
and in covenant with the Word of God, the
Bible. Satan does not give up until he is in perdition eternal torment - but then he is there - He is
eternally defeated - and his time is carefully
measured.
It is our time and as the children of the Lord - it
is eternal in glory.
There is no easy way - but there is away.

33

Pray in spirit against spirit
Pray in the flesh against the spirit

We can be at prayer meetings, we can pray correctly, but we get answers to prayer. Suddenly one day a light dawned on me about the case. What happens if I pray in the flesh, in the sensual versus the spiritual for prayer answer? I heard I said to myself, nothing happens.
We live in the New Testament era and far into it, we have passed the problems of the Middle Ages and come into greater light in the word. We see more and more of the Word, but it helps us a little if we just pray from the flesh toward the spirit. Don't we use spiritual weapons against spiritual enemies ...?

In Gal, Paul says to the Galatians: "Walk in the Spirit, and do not fulfill the lusts of the flesh.

For the flesh lusts against the Spirit, and the Spirit against the flesh, they oppose one another, so that you will not do what you will"

The confusion comes into the field
Here we see confusion also coming into the field. It is Satan out of the spiritual who comes with what we then accept in the flesh.
The Lord demands in His Word if we really want to serve Him, that He is Lord and that we then obey His leadership.

Then Paul's letter to the Romans is excellent: "If you confess Christ as Lord with your mouth, and believe in your heart that God raised him from the dead, you will be saved." (Rom. 10: 9)

Hear what Paul is saying to the Corinthians:

2 Corinthians "For our weapons of war are not carnal, but mighty for God to overthrow fortifi-cations,
As we overthrow thought-buildings and every height that rise against the knowledge of God, and capture every thought under obedience to Christ. " (2 Cor. 10: 5)

Fighting in the spirit is fighting with thoughts - thoughts are spiritual

Listen to what Jesus says in Matt. 9: 4 When Jesus saw your thoughts, he said, why are you thinking so badly in your hearts?

Jesus looked into the spirit and saw the thoughts. We'll see it again in:

Matt "But when Jesus knew their thoughts" (Matt. 12:25)

Further in Close" But a thought came to them about who was the greatest among them

But when Jesus saw the thought of their hearts" (Luke. 9, 46 - 47)

It is not difficult to read and understand, the revelation is up in the day. To a large extent, this is how Satan attacks and we must take him with the Word of God when we just make sure he is in the spirit, so that the Spirit of God in us in the word goes against Satan's spirit and wins victory.

What happens to most Christians is that they do not connect thought to the spiritual at all.
They think thoughts are thoughts, yes, they are right, but they are spiritual. All our thoughts, however, are spiritual. Thoughts and emotions are an important component of our spirit's life. They cannot be separated; every thought gives a feeling and every feeling gives a thought. Disorders of the mind when praying are demonic, disruptions in the mind are spiritually dealing with the aftermath.

Bring out your victories
in the spirit world

Deep Prayer in G.T. before the work of atonement under other conditions, led by the spirit of God Jehovah

We read from 1 King18,41-46 "Then Elijah said to Ahab, Go up now and have a drink! Because I hear the rain buzzing.

Then Ahab went up to eat and drink. But Elijah went up to Carmel's peak and bowed to the ground with his face between his knees.

Then he said to his boy: Get up to look out to the sea! And he went up and looked, and said, there is nothing to see. Seven times he said: Go there again.

On the seventh day he said, Behold, a little cloud, as great as a man's hand, rises from the sea. And he said, Go up and say to Ahab, Stretch and go down, lest the rain is upon you.

And in an instant, the sky darkened with clouds and with a storm, and there was a heavy rain; And Ahab went and went to Jezreel.

But the hand of the Lord came upon Elijah, and he encircled his loins, and ran before Ahab, even unto Jezreel. " (1 King 18, 41 - 46)

Here we see a fine example of going deep in prayer from the Old Testament under other conditions than we have today.
That does not prevent God from having his ways of exercising his will, as we see here through the prophets.
Elijah entered the spirit purposefully in faith and the expectation of victory came and it came. Of course, the Lord had taught the Prophet Elijah through training and trials for years before the great tasks and spiritual understanding came.

Here we see that he received divine energy over his physical body in such a way that he ran in front of the horses of Ahab all the way to Jezreel. Imagine what you can accomplish in the deep prayer that you are now heading into. This will be an adventure for you and you will no longer want to be in prayer in the spirit.

Deep prayer in the garden of Gethsemane
Let's go to Jesus in prayer in the Garden of Gethsemena

Luke.22,41-44 "And Jesus wiped himself from them as far as a stone's throw, and fell on his knees, prayed, and said:

Father, if you will, let this lime pass me by! However, my will not happen but yours!

And he came in fear of death and prayed even more fiercely, and his sweat became like drops of blood, falling to the ground. "
(Luke. 22, 41 - 44)

Here we see Jesus in deep prayer the last prayer before the crucifixion. He purposefully entered the spirit world, which he knew so well how to do. He had to do it to meet God and talk to him. This was so concentrated and powerful that his sweat became like drops of blood.

Here, Jesus made the final big decision, which in turn led him to Calvary's cross where he completed the work he had come to do - the wonderful miracle of redemption for you and me.

It is in the depth of the spirit and prayer that we get the answers and receive guidance from God.

Deep prayer on the cross

I repeat as I mentioned in previous chapters.

"Then, when Jesus knew that now everything was complete, for the writing to be fulfilled, he says: I thirst"

There was a tub full of vinegar, they then put a sponge full of vinegar on an isop stalk and held it up to his mouth.

When Jesus had received the vinegar, he said, It is finished. And he bowed his head and gave up the spirit. " (John. 19, 28-30)

Here in the last minute of Jesus before giving up
the spirit we see he is in the physical and the
spiritual. Here, the line of communication in the
spirit is open to God Jehovah while also being
conscious of the physical.

Jesus knew it was complete.
Here we see Jesus in the physically conscious
where he is monitoring the situation and see that
everything goes according to scripture so that it
is fulfilled.
Jesus now entered into the spirit
took on all the sin of the world, was made a son
of sacrifice for your and my sins.

Then into the physical consciousness
and says: It is finished and he gives up the spirit,
he gives his life for humanity.

The eternal last great victory is won.

35

There are 3 ways to get the prayer answers in the physical world:

No.1 We bind the relevant demons in the spirit and command them to leave man in the natural/physical world. We do this when we are in the spirit in the prayer closet.

No.2 We bind the current demon in the spirit and release the person in the natural/physical world as we are present with them.
We do not bind the demon here; it has already been done in the spirit world.

Ranked. 3 We are conscious of our state of mind while we are in the physical and bind and re-solve there. Then both are done there in the nat-ural/physical world.

These prayers always end with the signature "in the name of Jesus"

Disease breathe that attacks directly on the body

There is another ward of illness spirits that goes straight to the body, some from the outside and into the body, while others can again come via thoughts from demons and into our thought life, into our personality/soul and from there into the body.

We pray and believe with the obedience of faith to the Word of God in the Spirit and defeat the demons in the spirit and the result comes in the physical.

Do you want to hear the voice of God?

If you want to hear the voice of God, you must enter into the spirit world, you must understand that thoughts are spiritual. All the "disturbing" thoughts that come to you, no matter how ordinary and personal they may be, are from Satan who does not want you to calm down thoughts and feelings and discern, understand, where the thoughts come from.

It may take a long time, yes hours, weeks or months for the Lord offensively, before it begins to stabilize understanding of this for you.

You must be able to distinguish between the word of God in your voice/world of thought and your own words in your voice/world of thought. If you manage to put everything to a standstill in your emotions and thoughts, keep calm for a second, you will hear the voice of God. Now that you understand how to distinguish the Word of God from your words in your voice/thought, you are on the right path.

Remember for the Lord is 1 day like a thousand years, he can tell you what he wants in a second, what is the 1st second for you is approx. 21/2 day for the Lord (It is the calculation 1000 years is 1 day).

This is the reality

When you find the quiet second, then comes the thought/voice. There is no prayer shouts here, Jericho marches and tongues of war. This is the reality.

The reality of silence with God

The reality of the silence with God, where you are helpless and defenseless. You yearn and depend on hearing from God the Father, so that your life can be lived to its full potential in His will. Here in this first second, the Lord can give you all the information you need.

Find calm before moving on - pray in tongues

Hear what 1 Cor says. "He who speaks in tongues builds himself up." (1 Cor. 14: 4)

As you enter the prayer in this way, you may want to calm down before proceeding. Has something disruptive appeared or you need some rest in the advancement. Can you pray in tongues inside you and then you go back to work and work to bring thoughts and feelings to rest completely. Pray in tongues to work to keep all thoughts quiet. Even thinking that it will be quiet is and is a thought, it must also calm down.

Chamber of prayer in the Holy Spirit

Let's take a look at how to get into "prayer chamber prayer"

The Chamber of Prayer means peace in a small room, in the human being,

The proverb says, "The spirit of man is a lamp of the Lord, it searches everything within the human being." (Proverbs 20, 27)

Getaway and find peace
Mark says, "And Jesus said unto them, Come ye now unto me to a desert to a desert place, and rest a little." (Mark. 6:31)

Matt says, "Jesus says, But when you pray, go into your chamber; And when you close your door, pray to your father who is in hiding. And your father who looks in the secret will pay you openly. " (Matt. 6, 6)

Training - which takes a long time - close the gates of the senses - to put the meat to rest
Gal says: But I say, "Walk in the Spirit, and you shall not fulfill the requests of the flesh.

For the flesh lusts against the Spirit and the Spirit against the flesh; they oppose one another, lest you do what you will.

But if you are driven by the Spirit, you are not under the law.

But the fruits of the Spirit are: love, joy, peace, longsuffering, gentleness, goodness, faithfulness, meekness, abstinence,

Against such, the law is not. "
(Gal. 5, 16-18 and 23)

The proverb says: The spirit of man is a lamp of the Lord, it searches everything within the human being. " (Proverbs 20, 27)

Let's read Matt. "And six days after that Jesus took with him Peter, James's brother John, and led them away on a high mountain

And he was explained to their eyes, and his face shone like the sun, and his clothes became white as the light. " (Matt 16, 1-2)

We read further in Luke: "Jesus said to his disciples, I surrender the kingdom to you, as my Father delivered it unto me, that ye may eat and

drink at my table in my kingdom."
(Luke. 22, 29-30)

We look further at the Ephesians: "He raised us
up with him, and set us up with him in heaven,
in Christ Jesus" (Eph. 2: 6).
The psalmist says, "The Lord of hosts is with us;
The God of Jacob is our permanent city.
" (Psalm 46: 8)

The psalmist again says, "Against the might of
the mighty enemy, I will pray for you, for God is
my castle." (Psalm 59:10)

At the Lord's table
the table in the prayer closet

We read in Luke: "Jesus said to his disciples, I surrender the kingdom to you, as my father gave it to me, that you may eat and drink at my table in my kingdom." (Luke. 22, 29-30)

Ephesians says, "He raised us up with him, and set us up with him in heaven, in Christ."
(Eph 2: 6)

Paul said to the Ephesians, "And by faith in him we have access with confidence,"

We are now sharing company with Moses, Aaron, Nadab, Abihu and the 70 of Israel's elders who ate at the Lord's table on Mount Sinai.
" (Eph. 3:12)

Exodus says: And they saw the God of Israel; Under his feet there was a floor of transparent sapphire stone, clear as the sky itself.

He does not lift his hand against the foremost of the children of Israel, but they beheld God and ate and drank. " (Ex. 24: 10-11)

2 Samuel says: When David became king, he made a seat at his table for Jonathan's son, Mephibosheth: Don't be afraid, I will do good to you for your father Jonathan's sake ... you will always eat at my table. (2 Sam. 9: 2)

How to get to the Lord's table in the secret chamber of the spirit?

Now we are talking about stepping into an area of the spiritual world where God has the meeting place between him and us.

The meeting place of the Holy Spirit in the spirit world. If we are to enter here, we must move out of the world of the senses and the dominance of the flesh, and into the spiritual God of Jehovah.

Your prayer closet is inside you

There is a groundbreaking dimension that is within you, while at the heavenly place outside the universes. We have the meeting place inside us which is at the same time millions of light-years away, in the place we once travel to. Don't completely believe this, that's the way it is. You are entering a whole new life and a whole new dimension.

How to get into the prayer closet

To enter your chamber we must consciously cut off the ability of the deeds of the flesh to influence you and you may have to repent with all your heart, from parts of the deeds of the flesh that have been a problem for you. Then consciously close the entrance doors of the senses to you from the world of the senses around you. Now concentrate on God Jehovah and listen and look in the spirit.

The war is on

State your feelings and thoughts. Now the emotion and the influence of the thoughts on you must be completely rested so that you can be able to hear God's accusation from the Holy Spirit.

Now special thoughts are hammering your mind that you have to give deep concentration to let go. You have to let go of the thought that they will let go because it is and a thought.

This will be a workout for them that will take a long time, yes, weeks, months yes longer than that.

In this long process, you will begin to experience new things emerging in your prayer life. Experiences that come before you reach full victory, in what we are talking about here.

A whole new world will open up to you. Your experience and way of being in prayer will in many things be different from the experience of others. This is very personal and therefore very individual.

The psalmist says in Psalm 33: 9, "God spoke, and it came to pass that he commanded, and it stood there." (Psalm 33: 9)

Another place says
2 Peter: "But this one does not blind you, beloved, that one day is in the eyes of the Lord

as a thousand years and a thousand years as a day." (2 Peter 3: 8)

If we can manage for a second to be free from thoughts (which is spiritual) then the Lord is there with His speech and can tell you a thousand years of history in one second. Which dimensions, they are straight out Divine.

The battle of the mind is with thoughts and thoughts are spiritual
Eph 6.16 "Take hold of all this, the shield of faith, which will extinguish all the burning arrows of the wicked one" (Eph. 6:16).

So, we see the enemy weapons are thought arrows. He does not want you to calm it down so that you can hear the voice of God, but you can with training.

A spiritual campaign – A spiritual choice
To get through the last resistance in the moment, you must believe it is the Lord speaking to you, in your thoughts. Here come Satan's thought arrows again.

Here you have to leave things calm and focus on what you want to believe. If you believe it, you are inside?

3 7

Reflections

This book is the second of two, which deals with the same topic. This book goes deeper and will lead you into a reality you have to find your way. I guide you in so you understand which way to go. As I mentioned in the introduction, so much is included from the first book on this. But I saw that as important. In the last part of the book, I have included part of my book on prayer, which is published digitally. It's called "Prayer in the Deep."

I seem to see I have brought with me all the essentials of this book. So I said, I'll direct you to find the way yourself. Finding the way yourself is your learning process in the realm of faith. This will lead you into the consciousness of living in two kingdoms at the same time. The Realities of the Earth Kingdom and the Kingdom of God. These will be wonderful experiences and a wonderful life for you in your life as a Christian.

Tom Arild Fjeld

Has traveled all over the world preaching the gospel since early adolescence. In recent years he has written many books, which will be published in due course.

Current books for the time in history we live.

Follow him on social media, Christian TV stations and newspapers where he has meetings and teaching.

Join and support the service regularly financially or become a practical partner in it.

Contact us at www.tomarildfjeld@gmail.com
Missionary Faith & Vision
Account No. 0532.37.94229

Literature used in this book

1000 facts about space, Gyldendal publishing house.

Previously published books by Tom Arild Fjeld

How to receive the miracle of salvation in Norwegian, also published in Bulgarian, Romanian, Gassian and English

How to receive the miracle of healing

At the Barricade

More than one conqueror

Really free

Books recently published by Tom Arild Fjeld

Power wins the war

Get a loose box (Norwegian and English)

The hidden world

Dress up for victory

A warrior for Christ

He gave his life - nobody could take it (Norwegian, English)

Go out into the world

Impact in the spirit world

Victory over Satan

The Divine Realities

1 Daily breakthrough (3 months)

2 Daily breakthrough (3 months)

3 Daily Breakthrough (3 months)

4 Daily Breakthrough (3 months)

Reborn (in Romanian)

A New Life (Telegu; Indian Language) Specially written for 40 million Indian Hindu widows.

Tom Arild Fjeld

Brother Tom has traveled in 58 nations with the gospel. He started in this task at the age of 22. What has been a sign of his task from day one and which has always followed him is the healing of the sick, the expulsion of the evil spirits and the powers of darkness and the salvation of men.

In addition to his typically proclaiming preaching style to all types of people, religions, cultures, and peoples, he also has a service that teaches to all people. All of his teaching in speech and book form is a result of his walk with the Lord and obedience to the Lord's command to bring the good news of Christ to all peoples of the world. It all starts with the surrender and dedication to God the Father through His Son Jesus Christ.

Beginning on this walk of obedience, absolutely all spiritually important realities through the written Word of the Bible will begin to emerge.

Pictured is Brother Tom in the town of Plovdiv in Bulgaria. It's a rainy night. Weather and circumstances do not prevent God from doing what he wants, when his words are proclaimed alive and received by open, longing and humble people
Brother Tom is a proclamator of the Word of God and the Word has a powerful force in it to transform those who receive it.

Tom Arild Fjeld